Windblown

TAMSIN TREVERTON JONES

Windblown

Landscape, Legacy and Loss
The Great Storm of 1987

HODDER &
STOUGHTON

First published in Great Britain in 2017 by Hodder & Stoughton
An Hachette UK company

1

Copyright © Tamsin Treverton Jones 2017

Maps by Sandra Oakins

The right of Tamsin Treverton Jones to be identified as
the Author of the Work has been asserted by her in accordance
with the Copyright, Designs and Patents Act 1988.

A CIP catalogue record for this title is available from the British Library

Hardback ISBN 9781473656987
eBook ISBN 9781473657007

Typeset in Plantin Light by Palimpsest Book Production Ltd,
Falkirk, Stirlingshire

Printed and bound in Great Britain by Clays Ltd, St Ives plc

Hodder & Stoughton policy is to use papers that are natural,
renewable and recyclable products and made from wood grown
in sustainable forests. The logging and manufacturing processes
are expected to conform to the environmental regulations of
the country of origin.

Hodder & Stoughton Ltd
Carmelite House
50 Victoria Embankment
London EC4Y 0DZ

www.hodder.co.uk

Note:
Epigraphs are taken from a collection of poems
written by the author to mark the 30th anniversary
of the Great Storm of 1987

For Matilda, Kitty and Rufus

Contents

PART 4: The Road Trip

PART 5: Legacy and Loss

Prologue

15/16 October 1987

So, it begins

As a solid mass of cold air to the west of the British Isles drifted south towards a zone of high pressure over the European mainland moving north, the sultry remains of Hurricane Floyd high in the jet stream were chasing east across the Atlantic, 30,000 feet up. Polar air to the north, humid sub-tropical air to the south, an intensification from west to east, and the atmosphere was primed: a storm was inevitable.

In the Bay of Biscay, waves had been like walls of water for days. Off the coast of Spain, west of Finisterre, the *Markusturm*, an ocean-going tug, too far out and moving too slowly to change course, dropped heavily into every shadowed trough, rose vertically to every vertiginous peak. Wire hawsers lay frayed and redundant on deck, the crew sick and exhausted on their bunks. From his wheelhouse, the captain watched as two ships, his unbridled charges, disappeared into the dark, foaming distance, carried north before the gale like splinters on the gigantic swell. They were lost to the sea, their snapped towropes trailing, their engine-less shells rolling, pitching and falling sideways into the wind.

Humid air rose and turned to rain, leaving a vacuum close to the surface of the earth so deep that cold air immediately rushed to fill it. The earth turned, the winds turned with it, the depression deepened. The winds grew stronger and the storm moved north.

Across the Breton peninsula, from Quimper to Mont St Michel, power lines fell and crops were crushed; woodlands, enchanted forests, trees in their hundreds of thousands were systematically razed to the ground. At the seaport of Lorient and in the great marina at Cherbourg, 100 m.p.h. winds lifted sailboats and yachts from their moorings and threw them against harbour walls as the warrior wind twisted sharply into the English Channel.

But, like a necklace around the ragged English coast line, streaks of light cut through the clouds as Trinity House maintained its five-hundred-year promise to shipping and seafarers to keep the nation's aids to navigation ablaze. From whitewashed buildings, the lanterns shone: from headlands and islands, from crags, creeks and coves, and from formidable columns of granite that launch like space-bound rockets from wave-washed reefs surrounded by sea. From the lighthouses on Bishop Rock, four miles to the west of the Isles of Scilly, and Longships on the tiny islet of Carn Bras in the Atlantic, a mile and a half off Land's End. From Wolf Rock, the howling plug of phonolitic lava, nine miles off the south-westerly tip of Cornwall, and from the Needles, the jagged chalk stacks on the western tip of the Isle of Wight.

On the seafront at Hastings, where for generations fishermen have launched from the beach to drift, trammel and trap for herring, cod and cuttlefish, the sea threw the shingle at the drifting shoreline, and fishing families stood in anxious solidarity by their flat-bottomed boats, watching the rising tide ram the foreshore and batter the fractured harbour arm.

Heavy rain fell on All Saints Church in the village of Ulcombe, near Maidstone, where a group of bell-ringers, sallies in hand, practised in the draughty twelfth-century tower, the hallowed chime of their bells at sour odds with the jangle of the wind, the uneven peal echoing across sodden orchards of squat-stemmed apple trees, staked and fully loaded with unpicked fruit.

At Kew, the botanical haven on the banks of the River Thames, with its landscaped grounds and wide walkways, its orangery, glasshouses, temples and lakes, its historic collections of flora and fungi, the sodden earth could barely hold the roots of a thousand exotic trees and tender shrubs, imported from far-flung continents a century ago, shipped halfway around the world in glass cases or grown from precious seed and planted in careful clusters.

In a London park, men emerged from drooping cardboard shelters, wrapped in blankets, to stand beneath a desolate, band-less bandstand, nursing polystyrene cups of soup and cans of strong lager, shouting, laughing over the wind, as lofty plane trees arched, bowed and twisted above them.

And at the old rail ferry terminal in the eastern coastal town of Harwich, the *Earl William* – a disused car ferry and floating detention centre, her engines stripped down, her echoing car deck a dimly lit football pitch, one of her lounges a makeshift mosque – rolled and dipped violently at her moorings, snatching ominously at the thirteen ropes and two anchor chains that tied her to port. In the dank interior of the ship, asylum-seekers from boiling sub-Saharan Africa, from Iran, Iraq, Afghanistan and from the tropical island of Sri Lanka had already been locked into their cabin cells, portholes sealed against escape, fresh air and the bluster of a not-so-British gale.

Off the coast of Dorset, in the early hours of Friday morning, the storm turned and spun capriciously inland, raking the southern half of England in a cruel slant from Weymouth to the Wash. Behind closed doors and drawn curtains in houses across the country and in the capital, people lay awake in their beds listening to the scream of the wind and the pummelling rain as the storm came closer. Shop and car alarms wailed, drains overflowed, streetlamps flickered and went out.

PART I

THE MURAL

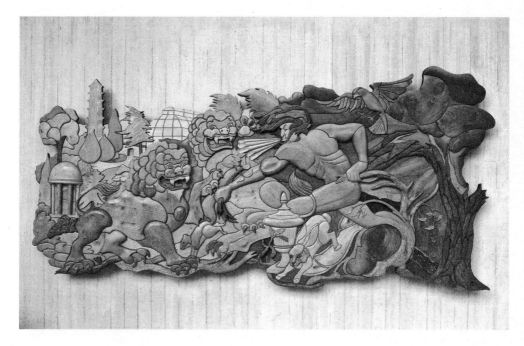

I

Gloucestershire

Spring 2015

pack me into your duffel bag
and drive me south again

I climbed the narrow staircase, pushed open the door and stepped over the threshold into my mother's spare room. The cooped air was stuffy and still, but streaks of sunlight fell across the sloping floor, gilding the clutter: the piles of cardboard cartons, the wall shelves crammed with books, the leftover rolls of Christmas wrap.

I knelt, lifted the floral quilt and squinted at the dusted mounds under the bed. I lay flat on my stomach, my cheek pressed to the carpet, pushed aside a pair of shoes and a suitcase and strained to reach a large low plastic crate, pulling it towards me. As I raised the lid, pastel crayons, tubes of paint and piles of paper released a long-held sigh of chalk, oil and vanilla, and I closed my eyes, breathing the memory of my father's attic studio that came with it.

I took his old paints and placed them on the floor. I lifted out a box of sharpeners, charcoal stubs and putty erasers, an A3 sketch pad full of half-drawn pictures, and an oval basswood palette with a thumb-hole, caked with hardened daubs of acrylic. At the bottom of the crate was an artist's folio, its brown ribbons untied. I picked it up and the sides fell apart, revealing pencil sketches, sheets of water-washed cartridge, unfinished landscapes with brushwork-blue skies, and a soft folder full of faded photographs, some black and white, some colour.

These were the old holiday snaps I was looking for: there was my mother with my brother and sister, there was me – over-tall and red-headed, a gap-toothed child in a fetching turquoise-towelling one-piece. And there was my father, in a field of sunflowers, seated at an easel, his back to the sun, or painting, bare-chested, at a camp table under a cherry tree.

We'd been living without him since 1998. My children remembered him only as a smiling face in a photograph, and I'd pared my memories back too, closing the sad door in my mind that allowed heart-stopping grief and loss to barge their way back in.

When he was alive, I'd hung from his coat tails, content simply to soak up the air around him, energised by his ingenuity, brushed by his creative brilliance, but too scared at the inevitable march of his illness to live in anything but the moment. When he died, the earth had simply dropped away beneath me and left me standing on a precarious edge. I felt as if I'd been turned inside out, like an old jumper, all hidden threads and loose ends exposed.

I could have done with his counsel and companionship these past few years as, bit by bit, I'd had to dismantle my family home in a drawn-out divorce that had left me ragged and insecure. I missed his cup-half-full humour, his dependable answers to all of life's questions, his small brave acts of parenting, that never ceased.

Almost twenty years after his death, I'd found that sifting through old photographs was a simple way to revive his ready smile, allowing me to look back with joy, at last, as well as sadness. I'd started looking more closely at his paintings again, too: the same old watercolours in the same old oak frames that had hung on my walls for years, admiring his bestowal of light upon a landscape, his ability to capture the thump and shimmer of heat, to express the purity of stone, the complexity of earth.

And when I re-examined his large square canvases, trowelled with their oily slabs of pigment, I began to understand that the wild stories they told, in their burned, brown language, were his invitation to me to start again: to look at the world anew, to see it from a different angle and in a different frame.

I was about to close the folder when I noticed a large photograph, mounted on cream card and covered with a sheet of crackling yellowing cellophane. Curious, I picked it up, carefully lifted the protective film, examined the glossy image closely and read the passage of typed text underneath:

The Kew Mural

Following the devastation caused by the hurricanes which swept the south-eastern part of England in October 1987, Robert Games, then a student at the King's School, Gloucester, went to the Royal Botanical Gardens at Kew in west London and helped clear the hundreds of broken and uprooted trees. His reward – a selection of wood from many unique and exotic trees, which he brought back home.

Terry Thomas was commissioned to design a 'Mural' depicting the famed Chinese Lions defending Kew against the evil spirit of the wind. Robert then cut and fashioned those retrieved woods to form this very large (*10* ft x *5* ft) and intricate interplay of grain, texture, colour and tone.

I remembered the Great Storm – how could anyone who was there forget it? I'd been to Kew in 1990, to see the grand carving in position, but I'd never seen this photograph before. The cellophane had done its job: after twenty-seven years, the image was still sharp and the colours still rich. It showed the huge wooden sculpture, an impressive panoply of polished timbers, displayed against a heavy bank of trees. The Victorian Palm House, the Chinese Pagoda and other iconic architectural features at Kew were unmistakable; the wind, a powerful god-like figure, every sinew in his strong, muscular body defined, was strikingly centre stage.

Immediately recognisable, too, was my father's bold, theatrical style. It was clear from the shaping and subtle relief of the carving that he'd understood the versatility as well as the limitations of working with wood, that he'd designed the mural to showcase the exotic tones and assorted colours of the reclaimed timbers.

The sights, sounds and smells of that legendary October night, almost thirty years ago, were as clear in my mind as if it were yesterday. Living in north London, in the top flat of a tall house on Parliament Hill, I vividly remembered the high-pitched scream of the wind, the trees whipping and waving on Hampstead Heath, the crushed cars on the tangled wet streets the following morning.

Now, those images were suddenly and inextricably inter-twined with memories of my father. I visualised him, leaning out of his attic window on the night of the storm, then perched on a stool in his studio during the rain-soaked days after, covering page after page with ideas and preliminary sketches, reimagining the devastation at Kew for this intense, muscular, meaningful design.

I took the photograph downstairs to show my mother, my mind a circus of connections, curiosity and intent. I asked her about my father's design, about the mural and about the young sculptor, Robert Games. Where was he now and how could I find him? How long had it taken him to carve the work? Had he done anything similar since? My head was suddenly brim-ming with other questions too, about the storm and its aftermath, its effects on people, on towns and cities and on the landscape.

It was as if the discovery of the photograph had set a ball of enquiry rolling rapidly downhill, with me running after it.

My mother held the photograph, nodded and smiled in recognition. More than anyone, she knew how my father's talent had lifted us and made us whole, but without him how empty life was, how fractured we'd all become.

She remembered meeting Robert and his father, Gilbert, when they had visited my father to discuss the design for the sculpture a few months after the storm and, laughing at my insistence, she promised to try to answer as many of my quick-fire questions about him as she could.

First, though, with the shining image of the mural in front of us, with the Great Storm as our marker and armed with our memories, happy and heartfelt, we decided to talk ourselves back to the beginning of 1987, that fateful, weather-filled year, and try to put the pieces of the jigsaw together again.

2

1987

hold your pencil to the horizon
and let it graze the paper

1987 brawled its way in with a glacial, bare-knuckle punch and a year's worth of fighting talk, and for the first two weeks of January, the country shivered in the lowest temperatures for a century. The freezing metropolis had already slowed to a crawl when heavy snow began to fall: fat flakes settling with icy intent, turning streets to lethal slides. From Cornwall to Kent, towns and villages were sunk in sunless drifts, and with the power down and the heating off, five hundred people died of hypothermia. The harsh weather continued through February and into March, with biting winds, snow and widespread frosts.

On blue-sky weekends, blanched air sparkling, I layered up with woolly tights and thermals, and wrapped an old pink scarf around my face to walk across Hampstead Heath, birdsong whittled to an intermittent chirrup, wind like a blade.

The frozen footpath down to the swimming ponds glistened, every stunned leaf on every sculpted stem a stainless white. Here, even on the coldest days, when gulls, coots and city cormorants huddled on frosted banks, lifeguards would break the ice for swimmers to dive into the frigid black water from a wooden jetty. I stood and watched as old men ploughed their blue-lipped furrows across the slick enamelled surface, before turning to walk back up to the top of Parliament Hill for a panoramic view of the city: St Paul's Cathedral and the Post Office Tower smoking with blown ice dust, like rimed monuments in a winter garden.

I'd arrived in the capital a couple of years earlier, a university graduate without a job, and I'd slept on friends' floors until I could find work and a place of my own. Eventually, I'd taken the flat on Parliament Hill and found a job in a deli in nearby South End Green. I'd work all week and, on Sundays, walk in gentle circuits around the Heath with my friend Victoria and her wiry lurcher, Spider, watching the trees change with the seasons.

I might have ached for the Cotswolds, the dark night skies of home, for fields and forests, fox bark and the drowsy, early-evening croon of the wood pigeon, but I'd left all that behind. I'd rolled my country childhood up behind me like a carpet to be one of the six and a half million people who lived, worked and played in the capital. I kept telling myself that I was on the cusp of something and that I needed to be in London to know what that something might be. The last thing on my mind was the weather.

In 1987, my parents were living in a small eighteenth century house in the hilltop hamlet of Littleworth, near Stroud, in Gloucestershire. My father's studio on the top floor was like a crow's nest. It had sloping ceilings and light-grabbing windows set into the roof at either side, and far-reaching views across the green valley to the south-facing village of Woodchester where, two thousand years ago, sun-loving Romans had planted bay trees, vines and sweet chestnut, built long, low villas and decorated their pavements.

Shelves on every wall of the studio were over-stacked with paperbacks, pamphlets and periodicals, with heavy reference books and hessian-bound volumes on Michelangelo and Donatello. There was a colossal plan chest, burdened by decades of paper, every one of its eight drawers obstinately shut and, beneath the front window, an antique drawing table, racked into position by industrial iron levers.

On every surface were sheets of heavy paper, water-washed in palest pink, green or grey, some blank, some threaded with fine lines, the pencilled suggestion of a landscape, a building or a tree. There were jam-jars, stuffed with brushes, all sizes, red sable and squirrel hair, a bamboo-handled Japanese calligraphy brush in soft goat, hardly used, and hundreds of pencils, all grades and a variety of lengths, each one hand-sharpened with a scalpel or Stanley knife. The soundtrack was either Wogan or Pavarotti: Irish bonhomie or Italian love songs, played at full whack on an ancient, battery-operated radio-cassette player.

The studio may have been a strategic roosting point for my wind-sniffing father, but for a man with a chronic lung condition, it was perversely situated. Doctors had forbidden him to smoke, but he was unable to quit and however hard he tried to hide his dangerous habit, the tell-tale ash was everywhere. Embassy and Peter Stuyvesant stubs, full tar, half smoked, were concealed inside drawers, in paper cups or shoved inside the baggy pictorial spines of old hardbacks.

To save himself endless short-winded journeys up and down the stairs, he'd leave the front door open. People yelled up from the lane if they wanted him and he'd poke his head out of the roof light and shout for them to *come on up* to his song- and smoke-filled eyrie. He would paint or draw anything for anyone, but his enduring personal passion was for landscape: for the Cornish coastline of his youth, the slate Snowdonian scenes of my childhood, the dunes and pine forests of the Gironde, and the perched southern villages of the Gard, bathed in their honeyed, Languedocian light.

In the middle of March, there was another polar low, another white-out. More heavy snow fell, stranding my parents in their house on the side of the hill for several days. People slid on their backsides down the lane, and above them, on the high, treeless plateau, on roads like scars, cars crept in cautious lines, the milky fumes shot from their exhaust pipes like hanging gardens of vapour in the cold, still air.

My mother filled hot-water bottles, turned up the heating, and stuffed odd socks and scarves into rattling gaps in the ill-fitting sash windows. Unable to get the car out to go shopping, she dipped her hands into the grim depths of the chest freezer, pulled up a lucky brace of pheasants, some frosted cranberries and a packet of chestnuts and, in an act of snowbound solidarity, invited all the neighbours round for supper.

Towards the end of March, as soon as the snow had melted, a severe gale swept over southern England and South Wales, killing twelve people, knocking out the power again and bringing with it landslides, floods and gusts of 100 m.p.h. off Land's End. In Oxford, a mature beech tree was ripped from its roots in the genteel grounds of Keble College; the 100-foot spire of St James's Church at Waresley in Cambridgeshire was brought down by a ferocious gust and, on 27 March, the Severn Bridge was closed to traffic for the first time in twenty years.

Two days later, under glowering skies, I made my annual spring pilgrimage south of the river to Hammersmith Bridge for the historic Oxford and Cambridge boat race on the Thames. There'd been a well-publicised mutiny[1] in the build-up, and as the teams lowered their oars to the choppy waters, the heavens opened and lightning struck the riverbank in divine disapproval.

In June, the re-election of Margaret Thatcher as prime minister for a third term was heralded with hailstorms in Suffolk and intense thunderstorms across Wales, the Midlands and the south-east. My father, rabidly anti-Thatcher, called me and yelled, incandescent with fury, his only consolation that the weather appeared to be of the same mind.

At first July was sunny, but by the middle of the month it

was raining again and for the whole of August the skies skittered with ill-disguised volatility: dry and very windy, with tornadoes in Rochdale, then very warm and very, very wet. In London, a delicate apricot bloom settled on window ledges and car windscreens as Saharan sand, blown north by the sirocco, was carried across Europe suspended in low clouds of unseasonable rain.

To escape the mercurial British summer, my parents performed their usual continental getaway. Chasing the light and the kind of dry French heat that loosens the breath, they crossed the Channel and headed south in their lumbering blue Peugeot 504. Deep down into France they drove, until they reached the baking byways and backroads of the Gard, where they settled for a month into a one-room, rubble-built house under cherry trees, with just a bed, a gas burner and a whistling kettle.

Too broke to afford a holiday that year, I joined them, swapping grey skies for sunshine and a free week in the Languedoc, travelling south from Paris on the TGV. My father came to meet me at Avignon station, towering above everyone on the platform, like a sunburned mountain in his loose light shirt, shorts and Panama.

And as torrential rain caused flooding from North Wales to East Anglia, and hailstones as big as golf balls ruined countless fêtes and fun days in Essex, I sunbathed, drank cold pink wine, breathed essence of willowherb, broom and mimosa and saw the world through my father's eyes, as I watched him paint the scorched landscape.

My parents came home in September to sunshine and blue skies; the trees had begun to turn but were holding on to their leaves. Then, in early October, the heavy rain returned with a vengeance: water levels rose, rivers broke their banks, and in Gloucestershire, the brackish waters of the Severn spilled into riverside fields at Frampton, creating sparkling wetlands that drew Bewick's swans in their hundreds from the wildfowl park at nearby Slimbridge.

By 15 October, the night of the storm, the British landscape was awash, the root systems of thousands of trees swimming in the loose earth.

That night, I stood at the picture window of my top-floor flat in Hampstead, the horizon a lowering blur of city lights. Beneath me, the forsaken garden with its twist of brambles and, beyond, the genteel grid of north London streets: Tanza Road, Nassington Road, South Hill Park. On the Heath, the beech trees were still abnormally full and as green as Eden, while ash, hornbeam and veteran oak, their sodden leaves a harlequin of terracotta and tangerine, bent heavily into the gathering wind.

A hundred miles to the west, my father leaned out of his tilting skylight window and, like the Cornishman he was, allowed the rain to batter his face, noticing a taste of salt in the wind. When fierce gusts threatened to rip the window from its wooden frame, he slammed it shut and locked it down. He lit a cigarette and repositioned the Anglepoise, turned up the volume on the cassette recorder until the voice of the lyric tenor drowned the whine of the wind, and, brush in hand, went back to his drawing table under the eaves.

3

Fish, Defoe and Romeo

waves steep as prayer hands
every temperate gust
a lion's breath
a prophecy

The last time a storm this big hit the British Isles was nearly three hundred years ago, in 1703, when an unusually fierce extra-tropical cyclone developed in the West Indies, blasted across the Atlantic and raged over Britain from North Wales to the Humber, killing more than eight thousand people on land and at sea. Bolts of lightning illuminated blackened skies, spectacular gusts carried men, animals and huge boulders through the air, blowing roofs and chimneys from houses and ripping trees from their roots. At sea, a fifth of the British naval fleet was lost, as were the lives of thousands of sailors and fishermen.

The meteorological records for that time are largely anecdotal, but the storm of 1703 has retained its infamous place in history, thanks to the author Daniel Defoe. In the immediate aftermath, Defoe placed an advertisement in the newspaper asking for people to write to him with their personal experiences, which he then presented in the extravagantly titled *THE STORM: OR A COLLECTION Of the most Remarkable CASUALTIES AND DISASTERS Which happen'd in the Late Dreadful TEMPEST, both by SEA AND LAND.*

Defoe's remarkable account describes a high tide in the

Bristol Channel that became a storm surge: seawater topped harbour walls and flooded wharves, damaging stores of tobacco and sugar. The wave seeped six miles inland, destroying eight hundred houses, drowning cattle and sheep in the fields and poisoning farmland with saltwater. Hundreds of vessels were lost at sea, and in the Port of London, Defoe observed around seven hundred ships, several 'with their sterns tossed up so high that the tide flowed into their forecastles before they could come to rights.'

Some were 'leaning upon others that the undermost vessels would sink before the others could float'. Fish were blown out of rivers and ponds, and windmills were destroyed by fire after turning too fast in the violent wind. In towns and cities, thousands of chimneys fell, and across the land, millions of trees were uprooted, woodlands laid waste.

The storm of 1703 flattened and destroyed everything in its path before making its way over the North Sea to Scandinavia and from there to the Baltic, leaving behind a shocked and traumatised population. 'I can give you no account but this,' writes Defoe, 'but sure such a Tempest never was in this world . . . No Pen can describe it, no Tongue can express it, no Thought conceive it unless by one in the extremity of it.'

The October storm of 1987 was of equal indiscriminate severity and caused a transformation to the British landscape not seen since the Blitz. The bespectacled BBC weatherman, Michael Fish, acquired a dubious new celebrity after making his now infamous statement on the lunchtime weather report on Thursday, 15 October, saying, 'Earlier on today, apparently, a woman rang the BBC and said she heard there was a hurricane on the way . . . well, if you're watching, don't worry, there isn't!'

Technically, he was right: the 1987 storm was not a hurricane. A hurricane is a defined meteorological feature of clashing temperatures found only in the warm, humid atmosphere of the tropics[2]. Our storm, though also the result of temperature contrasts, developed in the Bay of Biscay and was powerful enough to generate wind speeds that consistently topped 100 m.p.h. However, Fish's casual delivery and his failure to predict both the storm's savagery and its fatal trajectory across the densely populated south-east of the country meant that the people and infrastructures of southern Britain were spectacularly unprepared for what they were about to endure. When the country opened its curtains on the morning of 16 October, saw the utter devastation and began to look for a scapegoat, it was on Michael Fish that the media turned.

Severe weather had been predicted. For several days, forecasters had been watching the progress of two very different air masses that were moving towards each other in the atmosphere, one over mainland Europe, slow-moving, warm and drifting west, the other, much colder, out to the west of the UK and drifting south. The collision of pressure zones with such drastically different temperatures will always produce dramatic weather, as energy tries to level itself out across the atmosphere, so storms were expected. The remains of Hurricane Floyd, the last hurricane of the season and the only one to make landfall in the States that year, were helping to intensify that marked temperature gradient. Floyd had torn over the Florida Keys several days earlier, producing rip tides and tornadoes and killing a person in southern Texas, before rising into the easterly jet stream, bringing warm tropical air northwards into the western Atlantic.

Ships in the Bay of Biscay had been warned to expect appalling conditions where the two air masses were due to collide, and most had already made for the nearest port. Gale warnings were issued for the English Channel at 6.30 a.m. on Thursday, 15 October, followed by special warnings of severe gales at 10.30 a.m. the same day, as the storm moved inexorably north. Heavy rain was forecast but the accompanying strong winds were not, and although the depression was predicted to hit northern France and funnel eastwards along the English Channel, no one thought it would cause anything other than minimal disruption along the south coast. By 10.30 p.m. on the evening of 15 October, however, the storm had already stopped behaving as forecasters had said it would. Its volatile twist inland in the early hours of Friday, the sixteenth, took everyone by surprise.

Weather forecasting was in transition in the 1980s as outdated systems gave way to automation. Computers, satellites and automated buoys could predict a storm up to five days in advance, but the equipment was significantly less sophisticated than it is today. In 1987, the old computers at the Meteorological Office's headquarters in Bracknell were due to be upgraded the following year, and the costly, outdated international fleet of weather ships, which were essentially floating platforms for surface and upper air meteorological observations, were gradually being retired.[3]

Introduced after the Second World War and operated by a consortium of countries, the weather ships were originally positioned at important tracking points on the transatlantic air corridor in the Pacific and Atlantic oceans, giving navigational support as well as providing crucial meteorological data to weather forecasters. The weather ships floated in sea areas rarely covered by the Voluntary Observing Ships scheme (VOS)[4] and each of the original twenty-three sites was allocated a letter of the alphabet, from Able, Baker, Charlie, Delta and Extra to Mike, Romeo, Sugar, Tango, Uncle and Victor.

Each grid point required two vessels, and each vessel employed a crew of fifty-seven: fourteen deck crew, fifteen engineers, ten cooks, eleven radio/radar personnel and seven Met Office staff, mainly ex-Royal Navy and all men. The ships floated around the designated grid point for twenty-eight days at a time, allowing three days either side to sail to and from the station. Once at the grid point, the engine was switched off and the ship allowed to drift from the centre point (or 'middle-for-diddle') for up to a hundred miles in any direction. The power was turned on again only for the ship to get back to its allocated coordinates, or to maintain steerage in heavy weather.

Meteorological balloons were filled and launched with a radar reflector, their bearing and elevation tracked every minute until they burst and disappeared; water samples were taken in buckets, salinity levels recorded and plankton tows undertaken; Nansen bottles[5] were dropped, and bathythermograph[6] soundings taken daily, measuring sea temperatures down to 150 fathoms with deep bathythermographs performed on the sea bed once per patrol. If passing ships got into trouble, weather-ship crews were also trained to assist in search and rescue.

The data was important, but the weather ships were expensive to maintain; by 1975, the number had been reduced to M, L, C and R (Mike, Lima, Charlie and Romeo), and two years before the storm, in 1985, the French, who maintained the ship at Point Romeo, 47°N 17°W in the North Atlantic, decided that they could no longer justify the cost, so the ship was recalled, leaving a hole in real-time weather information for the area to the west of north-west Spain.

Then, as now, the Met Office relied on those voluntary observing ships to send wind speed and wave height back to their headquarters, where real-time measurements, along with satellite and other data, were fed into computers to produce the forecast. In the days before the storm, however, the weather warnings advising shipping to steer clear of the volatile waters of Biscay and the western Atlantic were so emphatic and so successful that, as those ships left the area one by one, another vital source of meteorological information was lost.

I installed myself in the Reading Room at the British Library, laboriously threading reels of fiche from the digital news archive onto clunking backlit machines, determined to read every article or report ever written about the Great Storm of 1987. I traced its tempestuous origins to Biscay. I moved with it on its raging journey north and east into the English Channel, over southern England, across the capital, to the eastern seaboard and out over the North Sea. As I was to discover, nothing that stood in the path of this storm was safe and nothing would be the same again.

PART 2

THE STORM

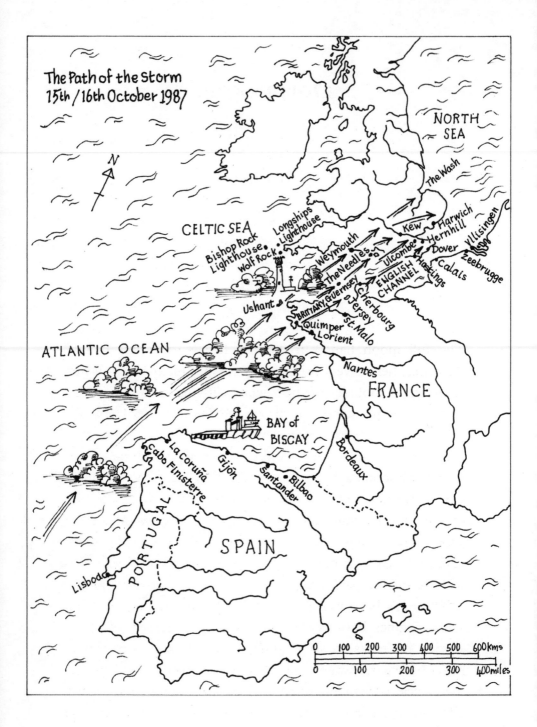

The Path of the Storm
15th / 16th October 1987

NORTH SEA

N

CELTIC SEA

Longships Lighthouse

Bishop Rock Lighthouse

Wolf Rock

The Wash

Kew

Harwich

Hernhill

Vllisingen

Weymouth

Ulcombe

Dover

Zeebrugge

The Needles

Hastings

Calais

Guernsey

ENGLISH CHANNEL

Ushant

BRITTANY

Jersey

Cherbourg

St. Malo

Quimper

Lorient

ATLANTIC OCEAN

Nantes

FRANCE

BAY of BISCAY

Bordeaux

Cabo Finisterre

La Coruña

Gijón

Santander

Bilbao

PORTUGAL

SPAIN

Lisboa

| 0 | 100 | 200 | 300 | 400 | 500 | 600kms |

| 0 | | 100 | | 200 | | 300 | 400miles |

4

Dover Strait

5 October 1987
Midnight

a cursed saltwater coffin
rusting, sulking, renamed,
her empty chambers and littered lounges
patrolled by the silted souls
of dead day trippers

The full moon hangs in the sky, like a threadless bauble, throwing her silver bridge across the night-black water, blanching a shoulder of sheer white cliffs in the distance. The tugboat captain stands on the bridge, leans forward over the control panel, checks his watch and squints through the glass panels at the unmistakable landmark. It's midnight and the car ferries will soon be docked, but even at this hour, the Channel's a busy two-lane highway. Up ahead, the notorious choke point of the Dover Strait, and in the narrow tideway, queues of super-tankers, tugs and tenders, heavy laden, sail slow and low in the water, though none quite as ponderous as the *Markusturm*, with its sulking payload.

The tug's been well prepared for this trip: its sturdy twin-screw engines have been taken apart and greased back into service, the tanks are fully bunkered with hundreds of tons of heavy oil, the freshwater reservoirs topped up, the galley stocked, the Decca navigation system[7] primed, the sea charts prepared. The nine-man crew, more than half of them Filipino, including the captain, a first mate, two engineers, a ship's cook and four deck hands, specially selected for their know-how, their vitality and their pluck, are already working shifts around the clock to keep the nips freshened, the fairleads greased and the oil lamps burning on the empty decks of the two un-manned ships under tow. Ahead of them, at least five winter months at sea: 13,164 nautical miles of torturously slow passage to the port city of Kaohsiung on the southern tip of Taiwan.

At this time of year, the long voyage down through Biscay, the South Atlantic, across the Indian Ocean and into the South China Sea, can be difficult, with raging storms expected around the Cape of Good Hope. But for the owners of the two ships under tow, the length and cost of the ships' transportation are offset by the enormous savings to be made in Kaohsiung, where vast economies of scale mean that it takes only three weeks to strip a 10,000-ton tanker down to its stinking shell. It's a job that takes the nearest competitors in South Korea the best part of two months.

Over the years, the captain has taken many ships to this filthy graveyard, but now tough new safety laws are beginning to bite for the Taiwanese shipbreakers, who've built their fortunes on salvaged steel, on scrapped aluminium and bronze, on discarded lifejackets, furniture, light fittings, cabin curtains and deadly cheap labour. For in the dangerous chaos of Kaohsiung, where vile waste burns on beaches and polluted fumes hang in toxic shrouds over the city, scores of men wielding gas cutting torches and sledgehammers work long hours for pitiful wages. They crawl in canvas shoes and bamboo hats over the rusting carcasses of cargo ships, ocean-going liners and damaged warships, gallons of crude oil still slopping in the tanks. They chew betel nut, drink *kaoliang*,[8] smoke on the job and work till they drop, which is, on average, at the age of thirty-seven. Once the new legislation is passed, the wharves in Kaohsiung will shut down within a year. The breakers will move their operation to China, where labour is still cheap and profits can't be squeezed by government regulation.

The captain knows that the ships will yield good-quality scrap: the *Gaelic Ferry*'s a floating workhorse, carrying cargo since 1964 and still sound; the *Flushing Range* is much bigger, a damaged and decommissioned passenger ferry, launched in 1980, her steel hull, funnel and propellers, her wooden decks, beams and berths only seven years old and still worth good money.

The captain checks his watch again, feels the solid thrust of the tug's engines beneath him, keeps the steering gear to midships and his course through the glistening strait at a steady but lugubrious four knots.

Getting the *Flushing Range* under tow to the *Markusturm* in the Dutch port of Vlissingen on the morning of 4 October had been a painfully slow operation: damaged, rusting and windowless, her orange hull dented and deformed, the lettering on her blue funnels crudely camouflaged, her lifeboats gone, she'd needed very careful handling. She'd been expertly turned and shifted, inch by creaking inch, away from her moorings, the crew standing aft, signalling to the skipper if the rope started to take up too much of the slack. When she was comfortably astern, the bight of the towrope well immersed, the *Markusturm* began to move forward at one, two, then three knots, increasing speed only as the *Range* straightened. Then they were clear of the harbour and sailing in calm seas towards the port of Zeebrugge on the Belgian coast to collect the second ship, the *Gaelic Ferry*.

The *Ferry* had been laid up in Zeebrugge's oily waters for a year, still charged with a cargo of obsolete link-spans from Southampton that had never been unloaded. In Zeebrugge's holding dock, the *Markusturm* crew bridled the smaller ship securely in front of the *Flushing Range*, corrected her trim, lit the oil lamps and rigged the emergency tows on both ships. Harbour staff gathered to watch the long-winded manoeuvres before the ships could depart, and finally the tug inched forward into Belgian waters, her lethargic double consignment to heel, the long voyage to the Far East under way.

The captain of the *Markusturm* was under orders to sail through the Dover Strait under cover of darkness. After that, it would take the convoy several more days to clear the busy English Channel and reach the open sea.

The first three days of October had been dry over the British Isles, but an overnight deluge on the third and a deepening depression moving eastwards towards the UK from the Atlantic had set the tone for a sodden month that would eventually make it the third wettest October in England and Wales since records began in 1727.

In the Channel, the *Markusturm* shared the slowest of the westbound channels of the busiest shipping lane in the world, with fuel barges under tow and dredgers as snail-like as she was. She was regularly overtaken by bulk carriers and general cargo vessels travelling at 15 knots: Lithuanian, Chinese and Hong Kong registered superstructures, Tampa-, Setubal- and Buenaventura-bound, their wide decks like boulevards, totteringly stacked. On the other side of the Channel, heading east, more container ships were on their way to Tilbury and Felixstowe, Ipswich and Aberdeen, or to Rotterdam, Bremerhaven and Antwerp.

In pouring rain on the morning of 6 October the *Markusturm* crawled past the town of Hastings on the East Sussex coast, where tall, black-boarded net huts stand at the foot of vertical, vegetated sheers, and fishing boats are launched from the beach in all weathers, metal keels scraping on the sloping shingle. At midday, as towns along the south coast piled sandbags against shopfronts, and commuter traffic around London came to a standstill in torrential rain, with all roads to Heathrow closed, the tug hauled her charges past Beachy Head in a bad-tempered squall. She trawled the shipping lane that shadows the southern seaboard around the busy ports of Portsmouth and Southampton, struggled past the red and white lighthouse on the white chalk stacks of the Needles in a Force 7 and negotiated the hazardous currents off Portland Bill and the Chesil Spit, the foghorn sounding every thirty seconds as the weather worsened.

Hanks of grey cloud hung at sea level and the green sea rolled. The captain slowed the engines as the towropes snatched and the trailing ships drifted in the heavy swell. The oil-skinned crew greased the fairleads and checked the ropes every hour for nips as the *Markusturm* turned into the wind for the wide-water traverse at the mouth of the Channel. The French isle of Ushant, fifteen square miles of rock and a sailors' landmark at the southern limit of the Celtic Sea, lay ahead and, beyond it, the west coast of France and the Bay of Biscay.

On the morning of 7 October, the *Daily Mirror* ran a headline on its front page, 'GHOST SHIP', and, with it, a grainy but unmistakable photograph captured from a light aircraft high above the cliffs that showed the *Markusturm* in grey seas off Beachy Head, the *Gaelic Ferry* and the *Flushing Range* behind her.

The 'ghost ship' in question was the white, windowless, engine-less *Flushing Range*, previously known as the *Herald of Free Enterprise*, a Townsend Thoresen passenger ferry that had capsized outside the port of Zeebrugge seven months earlier, with the loss of 193 lives, almost all of them British citizens.[9] Not since the sinking of the *Iolaire*[10] in 1919 had there been a maritime disaster, involving a British vessel in peacetime, with such a high death toll. The *Herald* had been refloated, repainted and renamed, but nothing cosmetic could ever conceal her grim back story, and seven months after the desperate tragedy

in the freezing waters off the Belgian coast, the accident was
as shockingly fresh in people's minds as the day it had happened.
Emotions were still raw. The *Mirror*'s article called the *Flushing
Range* a 'modern-day *Marie Celeste*', a 'shameful wreck', a
'crippled ghost ship'. The journalist noted the scars on the hulk,
the twisted walkway rails, the rear deck 'crazily bent', the company's distinctive logo painted over.

The bodies of at least four of the victims had never been
recovered from the ship's carcass and, as Townsend Thoresen
had no official record of the exact number of people on board
that night, there may well have been more. In the aftermath of
the accident, the company had received enquiries from across
the world, as relatives desperately searched for long lost loved
ones.

When the Dutch captain of the *Markusturm* had selected
his crew for the long journey to the Far East, he'd been careful

to choose unimaginative men. Although bananas, whistling and women are all regarded with suspicion by sailors, the *Flushing Range*'s gruesome history placed her in an entirely different league. The captain had to be sure that his crew would obey his orders at sea: that they would board the empty ship, day or night, as necessary, cross its stinking, windowless lounges on damp carpets layered with marine silt, confront the ghosts of the dead and missing that patrolled the rusted decks and crumpled walkways of the rusting hulk.

Despite the shipping forecast's warning of severe gales, the *Markusturm* left the maritime traffic separation lanes and turned south to join another busy shipping lane heading across the Bay of Biscay and down towards Cape Finisterre, on the north-western edge of Spain.

Biscay, eighty-six thousand square miles of ocean in the crook of France's west and Spain's northern coasts, is continually exposed to the relentless westerly winds that drive across the Atlantic from the eastern seaboard of the United States. It's a water-world of submarine trenches and seamounts, deep basins, canyons and abyssal plains. From its mesopelagic depths, devoid of sunlight and photosynthesis, bioluminescent krill, lanternfish, large-scaled ridgeheads, anglerfish and rattails rise to feed on phytoplankton at night, returning to the safety of the darkest depths during the day. Far out, blackfin tuna force flickering schools of scad, anchovy and gudgeon to the surface, the boiling waters signalling happy hunting grounds for cities of sea birds and for deep-sea fishermen.

At the 100-fathom line, where the outer margin of the continental coastal shelf begins and three thousand feet of ocean depth are lost in less than four miles, the waves become shorter and steeper. Winds whip the suddenly shallow waters into regular rages, mountainous peaks and yawning troughs – the ferocious storms for which Biscay is famous.

Many ships have been caught unprepared there and many have foundered there too. These days, experienced mariners will venture into Biscay only if they have a reliable four- or five-day forecast that can guarantee them good passage, for storms can blow up without warning, and the Atlantic swell that forms near the coasts makes many ports inaccessible. Knowing when to go and when to stay behind is an important and potentially life-saving decision for any captain of any ship contemplating a crossing.

Too far out and moving too slowly to head for port, the *Markusturm* continued her dogged journey south, the seas growing ever wilder, the ropes snatching and chafing, her crew falling over in zero gravity at the top of every wave, the two ships under tow drifting and yawing excessively.

In the dark early hours of 15 October, after several days and nights of exhausting vigil, all three vessels caught in the incessant climb and perilous drop of the waves, the stressed towropes snapped with a sickening crack. The captain watched as the ships disappeared into the churning oceanic darkness, carried north like leaves in the wind, away from the tug and back in the direction they had come. In sea conditions like these, there was nothing he could do to recover them. His urgent priorities were to reel in the parted wires, to stop them tangling in the *Markusturm*'s propellers and to keep the engines running and the tug nudging into the waves, heaving to until the winds abated.

Like jetsam, the derelicts[11] rocked and drifted sideways in the ocean off Finisterre, floating north-east for four whole days before the gale, to be spotted by the coastguard helicopter in the seas off Gijon, on Spain's northern coast, three days later.

The *Markusturm* managed to recapture her two charges in calmer seas on 19 October and after a port visit to check their seaworthiness, the long journey continued. Two months later, on 27 December, as the convoy rounded the Cape of Good Hope, a storm in the Roaring Forties gave the *Flushing Range* another opportunity to break free and she took her chance in the savage waters off the southern African cape. This time, the damage was almost fatal and she was forced to spend an extended period in dry dock at Port Elizabeth before setting off on the final leg to Taiwan, finally arriving in March 1988.

When the convoy arrived in Kaohsiung, the *Flushing Range* was towed to a scrapyard owned by the Jung Hung brothers, Jerry and Jonathan, who later revealed they had paid £800,000 for the wreck and a further £350,000 in towing fees.

Writing off a ship that had sailed for only seven years represented a huge financial loss for Townsend Thoresen, but the damage she'd inflicted on the company's reputation at Zeebrugge was incalculable: she needed to disappear.

Townsend Thoresen also brought forward plans to rebrand, changing their name to P & O Ferries (Dover) Ltd, under which they continue to trade today.

5

Needles Lighthouse

ISLE OF WIGHT
Thursday, 15 October 1987
Morning Watch 0400–1200

taught myself to knit
behind brass storm doors
on a tower rock station
six miles out into open sea

In his twelve years as a lighthouse keeper, Gerry had witnessed the sea in all its multiplicity of moods. He'd seen it ripple and shine in breeze-blown sunlight, change in a heartbeat from green to grey; he'd seen it lift and swell, pumped from below by briny bellows, he'd heard it groan and growl and roar. He'd stood with his back against dripping walls and felt the tower quiver and list, as waves big as houses pounded the brickwork with their salted arsenal.

In the summer months, when skies were clear and the sea calm, Gerry would spend the first couple of hours of the morning watch in the gallery, watching the dawn break and the sun take over from the lantern, but not today: at 0500 the sky was still black, the clouds low, the waves in Freshwater Bay heaping and foaming, the rain sharp as tacks against the small, square window in the watch room.

He completed his morning checks: he recorded visibility and temperature in the log book, noted the sharp drop in barometric pressure, the strong south-westerly direction of the wind –

without even putting his face outside, experience told him that it was blowing at 30 knots. He completed the chart and signed his name. He took a small notebook from his pocket, flipped the elastic that held it together, slid a pencil from behind his left ear and wrote, 'Wind round to SW7 – little hope of relief.' Ever since his first posting to Wolf Rock as assistant keeper in 1975, he'd always kept a diary, written a few words every day on the wind, the weather, even the foibles of his fellow keepers: you never knew when it might come in handy.

He made his way down the two open flights of steel stairs from the watch room to the kitchen, lifting his arms above his head as he did so to avoid touching the brass handrail – he'd only have to polish off the fingermarks later.

At 0600 Tony Isaacs, the contract boatman based in Yarmouth, called from his wide-windowed family home in Alum Bay to confirm what Gerry already knew: that the horizon was on the move, that the waves were already three feet up at the quay so they'd be thirty feet high at the tower, that he wouldn't be making it out to them today. Gerry allowed his heart to sink at the thought of being held over for the second time in a row. All keepers' observational faculties heightened as relief drew near and Gerry's were no different. He'd been monitoring the fore-casts obsessively for days, alert to every gust, to every tack and temperature change, but there was nothing he could do about the weather and there was no other way back to the mainland than by boat. A helicopter deck above the gallery had been under construction for months, but it hadn't been commissioned and, anyway, the keepers had all voted to maintain boat relief, rather than move to stations at Southampton or Bembridge.[12]

And there was always plenty to be getting on with: with his thumb and forefinger, Gerry lifted a dirty teaspoon from the table, rinsed it under the tap, dried it with a tea-towel and put it into the cutlery drawer. He wrung out the dishcloth and wiped the table, polished the wooden dresser, ran a duster over the bookshelves, then wiped the mottled mirror over the sink with cider vinegar and a clean rag. He stacked the chairs, lifted the rag rug, fetched the broom and swept the floor. He filled a bucket with water, detergent and a little bleach, lifted the mop and pressed it down hard into the wringer. After washing the floor, he replaced the furniture and started on the cooker, dismantling the grill pan, soaking it in the sink, wiping the grill with a damp cloth, sponging around the plates and drying them with a tea-towel.

At 0845 Gerry moved to the window, noticed that the wind seemed to have dropped slightly, perhaps to a Force 5, but that it was still raining heavily, hefty waves kicking the tower, sending arcs of spray eighty feet into the air and splatting the glass. He de-scaled the kettle, took the metal staircase down to the store room, filled the scuttle, hauled it back up, checked the dial on the coal-fired Rayburn,[13] folded the damp tea-towels and laid them neatly on the shining hotplate.

Long before the assistant keepers, Dave and Brian, joined

him at 1020, the kitchen was gleaming, the kettle was back on the hotplate and Gerry was already preparing an early lunch: boiled ham, canned carrots, potatoes, peeled and boiled, followed by reconstituted apple and tinned custard.

At 1045 Brian switched on the radio: 'This is a Shipping Forecast Special Warning issued by the Met Office on behalf of the Maritime and Coastguard at 1030 GMT on Thursday, 15 October. There are warnings of gales in all parts of the English Channel. Severe gales. Force 9. Soon.'

Leave the men at their table for a moment. Close the kitchen door, stand in the damp stairwell, note the runnels of condensation on the whitewashed walls, and listen to the wind, a giant's breath, rolling over a thousand miles of ocean, inciting fathomless depths to a monstrous swell. Hear the boom and crash of boulders on the sea bed, hauled and thrown as if they were mere pebbles against the base of the tower: 102 feet of untapered, un-breachable granite, sunk into chalk at four feet below low water, circular course upon rising course of grooved masonry, each stone dovetailed to the next, held together by hydraulic cement and anchored with gunmetal treenails.

Now listen to the men talking on the other side of the door: you'll hear the sound of both habit and happenstance, of three men thrown together and bound by confinement: three men so inured to the keen of the wind and the battering of the brickwork that they have long since learned to surrender to the elements, to live only in the present tense of the lighthouse. You'll hear their conversation ebb and flow, indistinct but companionable, consideration given, counsel held, as each man hears another out. It's like a muted canticle for three voices: melodic repetitions, silences, responsorial phrases and a slow, sacred resolve.

★ ★ ★

In 1973, the oral historian Tony Parker spent six months on remote rock and tower lighthouses, recording and transcribing a series of revelatory interviews with keepers, and with their families on shore. He made the stomach-churning boat trips to Bishop Rock and to the Longships lighthouse to live alongside the men, eat their food, experience their disorienting sleep patterns and share their stories of wilful incarceration. He noted the ruthlessness and unpredictability of the British weather. He observed the strategies the men had developed to keep themselves busy, to deal with delayed relief and to get along with each other in cramped, circular rooms for extended periods of time. A keeper, Parker noted, needed affability, self-reliance, discretion, and the ability to find ways to make the time pass: the intractable hours between watches were spent fishing, knitting, model-making, putting ships in bottles, talking on CB radio, reading in the gallery and, on rare fine, still days, walking in circles around the helipad, if there was one.

Living conditions in lighthouses changed little between 1973 and 1987. The perceived loneliness and isolation of the keepers were never the greatest challenges; rather, learning to live in close proximity with others was the real test.

In 1973, lighthouse living was still almost as primitive as it had been in the late nineteenth century: the keepers still occupied dark, round rooms with tiny windows, climbed spiral staircases to banana-shaped bunks, used an Elsan toilet and boiled kettles on a coal-fired Rayburn; they lit oil-fired lanterns, fired the fog guns by hand, spent two months on duty (or 'off') and a month ashore, then faced a difficult commute, as most lights were accessible only by sea and breeches buoy.[14]

The year before Parker wrote the book, in 1972, the lighthouse on Wolf Rock, the most isolated and most basic of all tower and rock stations, had been equipped with a helipad, to allow regular air relief to take place, rather than simply waiting for a clear day to effect it by boat. It was the first lighthouse of its kind to be given the upgrade that was to become widespread. Trinity House had been updating their aids to navigation, particularly lighthouses, since the end of the Second World War, but the process was interminably slow, physically challenging and very costly, and would take another twenty-five years to complete. By 1987, although the twenty-four-hour day was still divided into five 'watches', the duty rota had been shortened to the more bearable 'month-and-month-about' (one month 'off' and one month ashore) and oil lanterns had been phased out in favour of electricity.

It was not until 1998 that control of the light at North Foreland, above the perpendicular chalk cliffs of the Isle of Thanet, was passed to Trinity House's planning centre in Harwich, making it the last lighthouse to be automated and bringing to an end the era of the keeper. On the night of the storm in October 1987, however, thirty-six of the sixty-seven Trinity House lighthouses and light vessels around the British coastline were still manned. And although, for most keepers, storms were just business as usual, the men on some of the remotest tower lights in the Atlantic and in the English Channel were about to face the fury of the biggest storm to hit the seas around southern Britain for almost three hundred years.

At midday, the men ate in silence, as they listened to the general shipping announcement:

Thames Dover: easterly veering south-westerly 7 to severe gale 9, decreasing later, occasional rain. Moderate. Wight, Portland, Plymouth: cyclonic becoming west to south-west 7 to severe gale 9, decreasing 6 later. Rain then showers. Moderate or good. Biscay, South Finisterre: south-westerly gale 8 to storm 10,

decreasing 6 to gale 8. Rain then showers, poor becoming good.
North Finisterre: variable 4 becoming westerly 6. Showers.
Good.

At 1259, they switched on the television for the BBC's lunchtime weather forecast to hear Michael Fish talk first about 'the
vicious low pressure on our doorstep', but then to add, reassuringly, that most of the strong winds were over Spain and
France, that rain would affect many southern and eastern areas
but would soon clear.

After lunch, Gerry retired to his bunk and slept heavily for
two hours and fourteen minutes, waking disoriented at 1609
to the sound of Brian shouting to him from the stairwell. Tony
Isaacs had phoned again to say that, despite the heavy rain,
the sea had moderated, the wind was down to SE4 and he'd
be with them at 1830. The relief was back on.

At 1830, drenched and battered by the wind, Gerry and
Dave stood outside the tower on the concrete plinth ready to
board the ex-army aluminium assault craft that Tony had steered
expertly to the set-off from the big launch that was rocking
violently twenty feet away. As soon as provisions and two new
keepers had been offloaded, Gerry and Dave clambered into
the tin boat, their shouted greetings to Tony lost to the roaring
wind and the throttling engine. Surprisingly, the Isle of Wight
ferries were still running to schedule in the stormy seas, and
at 2005 the men were able to board the M/V *Caedmon* for the
short crossing to Lymington.

'Arrived 2030,' Gerry wrote in his diary. 'Train at 2056, got
to Brockenhurst 2110. Left Brockenhurst at 2138, got to
Waterloo 2245. Took taxi at 2250 and got to Liverpool Street
at 2310. Heavy rain and wind. Caught 2359 for Ipswich – slow
train, but at least moving.'

Two hours and four windswept minutes later, at 0203, the

slow train from London, buffeted by wind and needled by rain, finally pulled into Ipswich station. It was the end of the line, and a weary voice on the train's address system asked all passengers to disembark. Gerry stepped down from the carriage and was immediately blown into a wall by a veering gust. He pulled his anorak over his head and walked, with some difficulty, along the platform to an empty waiting room.

Standard British Rail: dark and cold, an overhead light-fitting with no bulb, a wall heater with its wires cut and a half-glazed door, clapping out of time against the jamb. In the middle of the room there was a large round oak table, on it a crumpled copy of yesterday's *Times*; along three of the walls there were low, slatted benches where Gerry curled up and immediately fell asleep. He woke after an hour, made a few notes in his diary, pulled a dog-eared paperback copy of Jerome K. Jerome's *Three Men in a Boat* from his bag and, completely oblivious to the sawing wind, to the flip and flex of power cables overhead, entirely unaffected by clattering doors and the rattling of loose-puttied windows, he lifted the bookmark and, for several hours, with full absorption, read his book to the end.

Much later that day, when he had finally managed to get back to his home in Norwich, Gerry completed that day's entry in his diary:

Waited for first train out. Trees and telegraph poles down every-where due to storms so no trains until about 1200! Had small breakfast, then wash and shave. Read papers and strolled about. Tried to phone home several times, but all phones u/s. Sunny periods but cold N wind. Snack lunch. Phones back on at 1300. Called a friend, but he 'caught up' in Southwold. Met up with a young artist who wanted to go to Norwich, so we decided to share a taxi (as NO public transport was available).

Several days later, he added,

Where public transport is concerned one becomes used to delays and cancellations. At dawn on Ipswich railway station I had no reason to believe the first train of the day would not provide its customary punctual service to Norwich. It was only when the signs began to be put up that all services had been cancelled at least until noon and, in the face of a complete absence of buses and taxis, that I realised something more than leaves or a small tree on the line had occurred overnight. Only marginal damage was detected during our shared taxi journey north into Norfolk and we were kept closely up to date with the astonishing headline news on the taxi radio.

I was just astounded that the Needles relief had plainly been effected during a brief lull in the weather before the storm struck. As ever, the success of the operation could be laid at the feet of our boatman and his pinpoint judgement.

I learned from my keeper colleagues that only minimal damage had been done to the country's aids to navigation, which just helped confirm our faith in lighthouse structures. Two weeks later, I flew into Southampton airport over the Isle of Wight where I saw for myself acre upon acre of trees lying flat on their sides. The result of such overwhelming natural violence was a truly humbling sight.

My fellow keeper, Tony Elvers, dined out for months on the story that on his station the PK (Principal Keeper), when arising on the sixteenth said, 'Storm? What storm?' He had slept undisturbed through the whole thing.

6

Hastings, East Sussex

Thursday, 15 October

7 a.m.

never once thinking that the land would take you

By 7 a.m. the Mermaid café on Rock-a-Nore, and the East Hastings Angling Club on the Stade, are serving cups of tea to fishermen who, on any other day, would be five miles out by now, each of their boats running six or seven fleets of trammel nets, each fleet dropped with anchors and weighted foot-ropes, the polystyrene floats with their brightly coloured marker flags bobbing and fluttering on the surface.

But no boats have gone to sea today: the unanimous decision not to fish was made last night, when a few of the men wandered down to the beach in sea boots and oilskins, raised their weatherworn faces to the wind, sniffed the air and confirmed the Met Office's forecast for Thursday: a strong south-westerly with heavy rain. Now, whining seagulls wheel and jitter against a black-slab sky, and windblown rain falls onshore from an open sea.

Rills of moisture trickle down inside the windows of the tea bars. The air, snarled with cigarette smoke, hums with brotherly discussions on tide times, tractors and tangle nets, on fish stocks, French trawlers and the thorny question of European fishing quotas. Outside, as the groaning sea rises, the boats lie idly on a ridge of auburn shingle that slopes steeply down to the water's edge. Upright, flat-bottomed, bluff-bowed and clinker-built, the thirty wooden boats – with their Kelvin engines, motorised winches and painted hulls, bulbous orange floats hanging off the gunwales, fluorescent lifebelts on wheel-house roofs gaudy against the thunderous sky – are representatives of the Hastings Beach fishing fleet, owned by the same Old Town families that have fished for cod, plaice and herring in double-masted trawlers, luggers and flat-decked punts from here for centuries.

Although diesel has replaced wind power and the horse-drawn capstans are long gone, the *Sandra*, the *St Richard*, the *Conqueror* and the *Golden Sovereign*, each with a style and seafaring personality of her own, are still shouldered to the water by strong men, scraped across the shingle every morning to where the sea nibbles the strand, to where the tide can lift and carry them out. At the end of the day, they'll surf back onto the beach with their catch, as they always have, keels grinding like teeth on wet stones, to be hauled back up onto the ridge by a motorised winch.

The men leave the tea bars and walk down to their sheds: a jumble of single-storey breeze-block structures with flat felt roofs that stretches the length of the Stade between the berthed boats and the black-boarded net shops. Even on days like this, there is always plenty to do: ground-ropes need making or reweighting, nets need mending and, if the rain lets up, the boats can always do with sanding, plugging and repainting. The Coglan brothers have recently raised their block shed up a level and they spend the day up there working on an old engine, running a power cable through a high open window, beach side.

By mid-afternoon, rain is falling heavily along this stretch of the south coast from Beachy Head to Dungeness. Some of the fishermen stay on the beach, while others go back to their homes in the Old Town, back to Scrivens Buildings, the dilapidated tenement blocks on Crown Lane, where fishing families have lived on top of each other and side by side for generations.

Dusk falls early and the wind strengthens, with gusts of surprising force that topple fish boxes, send piles of rope, old nets, floats and planks flying. The sea, thrashing and moaning, moves further up the beach, reaching the high-tide level at least two hours before time. As angry waves crash against concrete groynes and sea walls along the front, the whole town battens down. Even the seagulls disappear.

Darkness falls and the fishermen return to the Stade, senses on high alert to the taste, sound and smell of an unfamiliar wind. They don full waterproof gear and, heads bowed, gather in solidarity; sons, fathers, uncles, brothers and family friends, ready to battle in midnight teams to save the boats. Drenched by the waves and deafened by the screaming wind, they flatten the sodden stones with boards, run the winches at full power, press their bodies hard against the hulls and, booted feet sinking into the shingle, shoulder the vessels up the beach. At the end of the line they go back to the beginning and start again, making sure every boat is as far from the encroaching sea as possible.

The storm that took shape in the Bay of Biscay is moving north and east at a speed of 70 m.p.h., hammering the Breton coastline, flattening all the trees in a fifty-kilometre stretch from Morbihan to the Seine-Maritime, lashing the harbour town of Cherbourg, throwing itself at the Channel Islands, where gusts of wind measuring 110 m.p.h. are recorded on Guernsey.

At 2 a.m., a hundred miles west of Hastings, the storm makes landfall in Dorset and turns its dangerous attentions inland. Hundreds of trees fall, blocking roads and residential streets in Worthing. In the genteel seafront communities of Bournemouth and Highcliffe, the elderly and the retired watch the roofs of their apartment buildings take flight. In the coastal town of Seaford, east of Newhaven, a new beach, recently imported at a cost of £12 million, is washed away. In Christchurch, the cab of a fire engine, with a crew of six attending an alarm call, is crushed by a 12-ton tree, killing two of the men outright, an eighteen-year-old boy is killed when his car hits a tree in Salisbury, and a thirty-five-year-old accountant dies when a tree falls on his car in Petersfield.

Waves are twenty feet high in the Solent. Boats are thrown against harbour walls in Chichester. Power cables spark and fall, roof tiles fly, chimneys topple and mature trees are uprooted, like weeds, from pavements, parks and gardens. On the Isle of Wight, windows and doors are blown in, hundreds of fallen trees block the roads, telephone lines snap and flail and, on the eastern side of the island, the central section of the ninety-three-year-old Shanklin Pier is completely swept away.

In Peacehaven and Seaford, hundreds of tethered caravans in holiday parks crumple like cardboard, and further along the coast, at Brighton, one of the Pavilion's two-ton stone finials drops from its exotic perch, landing in a huge crater on the floor of the Music Room below. In town centres all along the coast, shop alarms are activated by the wind and display windows are shattered, creating splintered pathways for opportunists and looters, who brave the wind to walk away with thousands of pounds' worth of electrical equipment, porcelain and glass.

And in Hastings, as the fishermen continue to haul their boats up the beach on the Stade, the Early English Gothic spire of St Luke's United Reformed Church in the Silverhill suburb of the town is lifted and thrown through the roof of the north aisle, opening one side of the church to the elements. Two pubs, the Cricketers and the Robert de Mortain, are badly damaged by falling chimney stacks, and in Alexandra Park, where 1,500 trees were planted to mark the coronation of King George VI in 1937, more than twenty Scots pines are blown down, like skittles in an alley, by the hurricane-force winds. At the white-stuccoed Queens Hotel on Marine Parade, an elderly couple are asleep in a top-floor bedroom when a four-ton chimney crashes through the roof, taking them both with it as it falls: the wife, wrapped in a mattress, survives the three-floor dead drop, but her husband, carried by falling masonry, doesn't.

On the beach, the wind finds a way through the open window into the upper level of the Coglans' shed, removing the roof with a single gust. At 3 a.m. an old concrete winch shed, its sodden mortars loosened by the rain, collapses, injuring a fisherman who is sheltering inside and sending the roof high into the air.

As the storm passes and distant skies lighten to a coastal grey, a man walks his dog along the breathless, birdless battleground of a beach, the shingle scattered with plastic crates, cuttle traps, fish boxes, flags, floats and planks. The tide is receding, blanketing the pebbles with a glutinous white foam. The soaked, exhausted fishermen are back in the tea bar, their work done.

The dog gallops lopsided, nose down, up the beach towards the net shops, away from his master, who's kicking stones into the sea at the water's edge. Scuttling among unfurled nets and piles of rope, the dog lifts his leg against the tyre of a rusting tractor and snuffles around the collapsed, roof-blown winch shed. When the walker hears barking, he turns and crunches up the beach to where the felted roof lies at an awkward angle on the ground. The dog circles and whines as his master lifts the edge of the sopping timbers to find the inert body of a man lying in a puddle of blood.

The roads up to the Royal East Sussex Hospital are blocked by fallen trees and no ambulances can make it down to the

Stade to collect the casualty, but the fishermen lift their man, even though they know he's gone, lay him with care on a flat-bed truck and take him to the hospital themselves, stopping every few yards to clear debris from the tarmac.

Wrong place, wrong time. Jimmy Read, husband, father, best mate, boy ashore and the strongest man on the Stade: a fisherman with enough muscle to tow a shrimp trawl behind a rowing boat, who could shoulder a boat to water single-handed, who could ride up Crown Hill on a butcher's bike without ever taking his backside off the saddle, who'd spent all night saving the boats with his brothers and was sheltering behind the winch shed when that gust came. He never knew what hit him.

7

Lincoln's Inn Fields

CENTRAL LONDON
Thursday, 15 October
8 p.m.

slender gingko, judas, downy birch,
I know these trees in all seasons,
wilful wanderers like me,
their shallow roots in city soil

Jeremy stands in the shelter of the underpass and looks out at the night: lamplights flicker phosphorescent against a storm-black sky and the rain falls in a cruel, urban slant. Overhead power cables whistle and whine, while a metal dustbin lid clatters and rolls down the empty street. He pulls his fur-lined parka hood over his head, zips the coat up to his neck, folds the flare of his jeans into a pair of cycle clips and makes a dash for the bike chained to a nearby lamppost.

Launched by the strong southerly wind, lashed by rain, he leaves the South Bank, cycles through oil-streaked puddles around the Bull Ring, cruises over Waterloo Bridge, is powered up the gentle incline around the Aldwych and pedals hard through a zigzag of streets – Houghton, Portugal, Portsmouth – until he reaches the swaying green corner of Lincoln's Inn Fields, where huge trees flex and bend, limber as saplings in the gathering wind. He swerves through a pair of iron gates, negotiates a footpath, slippery and thick with fallen leaves, and skids to a halt in front of the bandstand.

Lincoln's Inn Fields, with its company of flaking plane trees, is the largest of London's public squares, its tall historically significant buildings occupied by lawyers and surgeons, its netball courts and grassy shade once a place for office workers to spend an hour at midday, but not any more: this worn, stinking patch of ground is now almost entirely the preserve of the homeless, a bleak, sodden, unstructured, fragile, sagging township of boxes, full of menace and volatility.

Jeremy steps up onto the platform to join a huddle of men, worsted collars up, mittened hands shaking, sheltered somewhat from the rain, but not from the pounding wind. Acknowledged with nods and murmurs, he smiles and banters with them about the weather, barely registering the sour stench of urine, the fermented tang of cheap alcohol, the smell of cigarettes and wet cardboard. He moves easily among them, notices the daily toll that drink, drugs and sleeping rough are taking, and offers hostel beds, tonight of all nights, to those who are coughing or unwell. He wishes there was more he could do, but with hostels already at capacity and numbers on the streets rising every day, his options, and theirs, are increasingly limited. By the toilets, a couple of buffeted Buddhists attempt to serve soup, holding onto towers of foam cups with one hand, flattening their flapping orange robes with the other.

He's been an outreach worker on the front line for three years now, on the streets every night of the week, from 7 p.m. to 1 a.m. His charges are the disturbed, the displaced, the rootless, the addicted and the abused. They live in 'bashes', semi-permanent dwellings fashioned out of plastic, board and corrugated metal in the concrete tunnels beneath the Queen Elizabeth Hall, underneath the Bull Ring at the end of Waterloo Bridge and here in Lincoln's Inn Fields.

Whether mentally ill, ex-army, just out of prison or simply fallen foul of Margaret Thatcher's welfare and benefit cuts, they sleep in their hundreds, in lines, in bags, under broad-sheets, in boxes and bins, the scrapings of the street, surrounded by rats, filth and fear. They beg, drink, smoke, shoot up, fight and sleep; they trudge from one dispiriting day centre in Victoria to another in St Martin-in-the-Fields or to the American Church in Tottenham Court Road; they spend hours in the foyer at the Festival Hall, follow the Salvation Army early-evening soup runs, or make their way to the Silver Lady in the Temple, where an elderly widower carries out his dead wife's wish that hot pies be handed to the homeless twice a week.

Until he'd answered a newspaper advert that offered free accommodation and nine pounds a week to volunteers willing to live in a hostel in west London, Jeremy hadn't known what he wanted to do with his life, or even what homelessness was. But within weeks he'd seen that he could make a difference, that he could help the residents just by talking to them. He went on to work with homeless teenagers in King's Cross, kids stamped on by poverty and abuse, their lives already defined by brutal lack of interest and opportunity. He didn't have to listen for long to their shocking stories to know that life is not an even playing field, to understand the depressing cycles of dereliction and despair. By the time he took the job with Thames Reach in 1984, he'd already cut a deal with himself: he knew he'd never get rich, but working with the homeless was what he wanted to do.

And the all-too-familiar feelings of frustration, sorrow and helplessness are balanced by a genuine affection for and interest in the people he meets on the streets, people who constantly challenge his notions of what homelessness means and what it looks like: the man who wears a suit and tie, carries a briefcase and sleeps in a phone box, the woman who reads Dickens, the girl who sleeps in the trees, the man who quotes Shakespeare, the Scotsman who crashes out on the bandstand and rolls down the steps in his sleep – even the heroin addict who beats him up, breaks his nose and chases him out of the park.

But after three years' listening to their stories, keeping a weather eye on the very vulnerable, on the shifting friendship groups, the drinking cabals and the dealers, after watching tensions rise, fires burn and fights develop, he's beginning to wonder when change will come, when he will have more than just words to offer, and how much longer these cities of cardboard can be allowed to exist.

And now, at midnight, the rain like a curtain, the wind screaming in dangerous Dervish circles around the bandstand, he's increasingly anxious about the safety of the men in this square. He repeats his offer of a dry hostel bed to a couple of the older ones, who pointedly shrug their shoulders, shake their heads and turn away, disappearing into the darkness to crawl under their cardboard shelters beneath the trees.

Finally, as more rain falls, as the wind grows ever wilder and, concerned that he may not make it home, he reluctantly unlocks his bike and pedals with difficulty away from the Fields, on city streets slimy with tawny leaves and fallen boughs. At 1 a.m., crossing Westminster Bridge, he's thrown to the ground by a sudden shrieking, swerving gust of wind. Dazed, nose bleeding, palms badly grazed, he sits and watches as his bike is lifted, like a feather, by ghostly fingers and thrown to the other side of the road, where it lands with a crash and a sickening scrape of metal on the glistening asphalt.

Just before 4 a.m., two young policemen stagger along the northern edge of Lincoln's Inn Fields on their regular night-time beat, belted, booted and helmeted against the rain, their professional poise shattered by a wind that is by now a boulder-like force that shoves them in all directions, sends them stumbling, hurtling into walls and railings, tripping over fallen trunks and heavy green boughs.

A shout for help sets them running. They round the north-eastern corner of the square and enter by the iron gates to find a cluster of men clinging to each other, their already haunted faces lined with panic and fear, pointing to where a colossal plane tree lies horizontal, like a still-breathing casualty on a stretcher of dripping greenery. Its upturned root plate is fifteen feet in the air, a helix of flailing tails like a gorgon's head, its pale trunk at a shallow angle to the ground, almost luminescent in the lamplight.

Using a truncheon, one of the policemen thrashes forwards, stamping on split branches and wind-thrown wads of wet leaves, shining his torch on the tangle of vegetation until the beam catches a glint of man-made fibres buried deep beneath. He shouts over the wind to his companion, who immediately reaches for the radio pager clipped to his lapel.

The Bloomsbury One ambulance team have been on duty since 11 p.m. and have already responded to an unprecedented number of emergency calls when they receive the message from Lincoln's Inn Fields at 4.03 a.m. As they drive into the square at the northern end, they are flagged down by a group of wind-whipped men wrapped in blankets and clutching cans of lager.

The ambulance men zip up their jackets, put their heads down and fight the gale into the park to where the policemen have made attempts to clear them a passage to the body of a man in a sports jacket and a pair of jeans, lying on his side, knees drawn up to his chest, legs covered with leaves and branches. They check for two radial pulses, then the carotid, but the man's chest is not moving, his body is cold.

The streetlamps flicker suddenly and go out, abandoning the ambulance men, the policemen and the crushed body to the howling, sap-filled gloom. The policemen hold their torches high as the ambulance men struggle to release the dead man from the tree's mortal grasp, straightening his legs, placing him with care on a carrying sheet. They cover his face and bear him to the van, flanked by desolate rows of silent grey men, who let their arms hang and their heads drop.

One of the policemen shouts, 'Anyone know this man? What's his name?' But the wicked wind steals his words, lifts them, turns them, tilts them and sweeps them away, high into the speeding stratosphere.

8

Hernhill & Ulcombe, Kent

Thursday, 15 October
9 p.m.

Eastern steppe to northern wold;
England's harvest, Eden's gold.

On the upper level of an old oast house at Mount Ephraim, near Hernhill in Kent, a family of fruit pickers, Otis and Dolly Smith and their seven children, are sitting on the slatted floor, cradling mugs of strong brown tea, listening warily to the howl of the wind outside.

The oast is sturdily built of yellow stock, with red-brick quoins and weatherboard gables, and it sits in a hollow at a junction of shale farm tracks among apple orchards. Its roof once boasted two enormous cowls, its interior two huge kilns, but when tastes changed, when people began to drink lager instead of beer and as continental hops began to overwhelm the domestic market, Mount Ephraim, like many UK farms, tore down the hop poles and trellises and planted fruit trees instead. The cowls and kilns were scrapped, a new roof was added and the oast house was used for storing ladders, grabbers, trugs, tools, and hundreds of wooden fruit crates instead.

The Smiths have been working the Hernhill orchards for years. They spend their winters in Southampton, where Otis deals in scrap, before setting off in spring, the children's schooling abandoned, for a round of fruit and vegetable harvests that will take them through to autumn. To Yorkshire first, to a cluster of dark, dry forcing sheds on Ackworth Moor Top, pulling smooth, crimson rhubarb shoots by candlelight. Then to Hampshire, for early watercress, cutting the pale submerged stems and peppery leaves from their gravel beds, arranging twine-tied handfuls of green on layers of crushed ice. From there to Kent, kneeling for strawberries, climbing for hops and reaching for apples, parents and children alike. For six months, they live like casual kings: they sleep like logs on straw bedrolls on the drying floor of the old oast house, eat windblown fruit, wash in running streams and gather scented apple sticks for their open fires.

The Dawes dynasty, who have owned and worked the sheltered, fertile land at Mount Ephraim for more than three hundred years, built their imposing family mansion on the proceeds of colonial shipping in 1876. The house is surrounded by woodland, topiary and ornamental lakes, by genteel rose terraces, yew hedges, a Japanese rock garden, and by 150 acres of apple and pear orchards, intensively planted in two- and three-bed rows for maximum yield.

The glorious centrepiece at Mount Ephraim is a gigantic, multi-stemmed *Macrocarpa,* a flat-topped cypress that dominates the lawn in front of the house. For several generations, the Dawes children have shunned all prefabricated climbing frames in favour of this *grande dame* they call the Victory: they've hidden in her, swung from her spreading boughs, acted out Robin Hood, *The Jungle Book* and Blackbeard, the pirate, high in her dense green foliage; and though their mothers curse the sap that sticks to skin and clothing, nobody can imagine the garden without her.

On the same wet Thursday evening, twenty miles south-west of Hernhill, the bronze bells high in the square tower of All Saints, Ulcombe's ragstone church, are singing their sacred, solemn song. The six bells, shaped, sounded and hung four hundred years ago by Joseph Hatch, bell-founder and local man, have dappled the hills and hollows of this Kentish settlement with their monastic tones for generations: new life, marriage, death and prayer, Ulcombe's ancient history, her pre-Christian past, her present; the circle of life tolled in the round by a plosive treble, a plangent tenor and four plain notes in between.

For young Charles Tassell and his fellow ringers, the weekly practice in the whitewashed belfry is as much a chance to catch up on village news as it is to ring a straightforward Plain Bob Minor or a more challenging Stedman Doubles. Conversations begun between peals will continue in the Provender pub afterwards, over a pint of Bishop's Finger and a large plate of chips.

Last to leave the church at 9 p.m., Charles switches off the lights, locks the solid oak door and jogs along the path through the graveyard, taking a moment to shelter under the dripline of a monumental yew tree, heavy raindrops sliding off its waxy needles. He finds a herringbone flat cap in the pocket of his jacket, pulls it on, runs to the car and drives through the lanes to Pye Corner to join the other ringers at the pub.

The Tassell family have farmed five hundred sunny acres in Ulcombe since the 1870s, raising hops on the fertile, well-drained soil, watching the stout-stemmed bines rise and climb, the decorative cones burgeon in lime clusters. Charles's great-grandfather adapted the long barn to stowage, installing tall, circular chimneys and a charcoal-fired kiln. At harvest time, entire families would arrive in droves, on late-night trains from Stepney, Shadwell, Shoreditch and Bow, trading their tenement flats for hastily built hopper huts, swapping smoke, grime and city stench for the sweet smell of malt, the pungent heat of the oast house and three months' hard graft in open fields.

Hop husbandry declined across Kent in the 1960s, but by

then, the Tassells had already turned their steep, sloping acreage to arable and fruit, growing strawberries on the sandstone heights, cereals on clay below and rows of apple trees on the sandy loam in between. In the 1970s the farm grew 150 acres of Bramley, Spartan, Cox's and Discovery, planted, picked and packed by scores of local people, stacked in crates in the corrugated cold store and sold wholesale at the fruit markets.

Charles and his brother grew up in the seventeenth-century farmhouse next to the church, its simple earthen floors lined with red brick, low ceilings braced with sooty timbers, crests carved into the corners of the blackened oak door frames, and a bright red oil-fired Aga on full pump, summer and winter. It's to the family farm that Charles has returned, after three years at college, to work with his father and brother on the land, every tilt, tip and slide of which he knows so well.

After a wet autumn, the Tassell apple orchards are still unseasonably green; at the bottom of the hill, in long rows planted east to west, eight acres of Bramleys have already been picked, their low, empty branches splayed flat, like gnarled fingers on an open palm. But in the exposed field above the house, behind a poplar windbreak, a newly planted orchard, its slender trees only three years old and eighteen months from fruiting, stands alongside an older orchard of Bramleys planted north to south, still in leaf and fully loaded.

At 10.30 p.m., the ringers settle up and leave the Provender, remarking to each other as they run through the rain to their cars how warm it has become, indeed, how very much warmer it is outside now than it was when they first arrived.

The marked increase in temperature that Charles and the bell-ringers had noticed was one of the striking features of the storm, as it tracked north-east across the cold southern corner of England. Temperatures rose by up to ten degrees in a short time, as warm air sitting on the continent was pulled across by the spinning storm. Temperature increases of more than 6°C (43°F) in an hour were recorded in many places south of a line from Dorset to Norfolk: at Heathrow airport, the temperature rose by 7°C (45°F), the greatest one-hour temperature rise in thirty-seven years. At South Farnborough in Hampshire, the temperature rose from 8.5°C (47°F) to 17.6°C (64°F) in just twenty minutes, and behind the storm, there was a sharp fall in temperature as the cold front passed and the winds swung round to the north-west, bringing cooler air across the UK.

It's now known that some of the worst damage caused in the south-east was due to the sting jet, a meteorological phenomenon understood and discussed in research circles at the time, but not yet included in your average weather forecaster's training or vocabulary. A sting jet occurs when cold dry air descends into storms high in the atmosphere, evaporating as it falls, cooling and drying the air and adding energy, which in turn brings stronger winds. It can take three or four hours for a sting jet to descend from high altitude, and when it reaches the ground, hammering gusts of up to 100 m.p.h. can last for an hour or two before the storm retreats. On satellite pictures, a sting jet has a distinctive appearance: a hook-shaped cloud curling into the back of a storm, just like the sting in a scorpion's tail.

As the storm crossed southern England in the early hours of 16 October, and as the vicious winds ahead of the storm caused catastrophic damage, the sting jet behind them caused even more, delivering its final parting kick after a deceptive moment of calm as the storm moved on.

If the trees in the Ulcombe orchards had been planted with a different orientation, if the ground hadn't been waterlogged, if the wind had been blowing from a different direction and with less force, would the crop have survived?

If the roof on the old oast house at Mount Ephraim had been more securely fixed when the circular cowls were removed, would it have held, even in the face of the 100 m.p.h. gusts? And could anything have saved the cypress tree, the Victory, standing unsheltered and alone in stately grandeur, as she did, in front of the house?

When Charles and his father surveyed their land on the morning of Friday, the sixteenth, during a brief period of blue-sky calm before the next rainfall, they found that the entire orchard of newly planted trees above the house had been lifted, like twigs, sent flying over the tall poplar windbreak and dumped in a neighbouring field. In the lower field, every tree had been pushed carelessly to one side and the small but sturdy Bramleys were now lying at a 45° angle to the ground, most of their roots lifted, the gap between each row shifted by five full feet.

At Hernhill, too, entire apple and pear orchards lay on their sides, thousands of fruiting trees over many acres elbowed maliciously by the same wind that had lifted the long, heavy roof off the oast in one piece and shoved it on its gutter edge to one side of the building. And the same wind had dealt the Victory her mortal blow, pulling her up by the roots, sending her crashing to earth, her ragged root plate fifteen feet high in the air, a pit four feet deep in the sodden lawn.

Unlike the Victory, Otis, Dolly and the children had a lucky escape, scrambling to get out of the oast house only minutes before a blast of wind tore the roof from its fixings. The family ran in terror to the big house, where they were discovered the following morning in sleeping rows in a public tea room, too shocked to speak of their ordeal.

Across the entire fruit-growing south-east of the country, every farm suffered similar losses: barn roofs were lifted, tiles were blown away, ragstone and sandstone walls collapsed, and thousands upon thousands of acres of apple and pear trees, most of them still heavy with fruit and foliage, were pushed to one side or ripped savagely from their roots. When the government subsequently announced compensation for fruit farmers of £1.50 per lost tree, some farmers chose to grub out the damaged orchards and start again (although the price of trees then rose by the same amount in response to the huge and sudden demand). Other farmers tried to right the windblown trees in the damaged orchards, lifting and staking each one back to vertical, pushing broken roots into the ground, but with limited success: few trees treated in that way lived for long.

The Dawes family were philosophical in the aftermath of the storm: the orchards at Mount Ephraim had suffered, but not as badly as those sited on Ulcombe's rising contours or, indeed, as the orchards around Sevenoaks, which took the full blast of the sting jet. For some badly damaged fruit farms it was decision time: those who had not embraced new techniques or invested in new equipment now faced huge replanting costs as well as having to update their orchards in the aftermath of the storm. Over the next few years, the fruit industry would face further significant challenges to both production and supply. Only the fittest would survive.

On the morning after the storm, an Australian opera singer who was staying with the Dawes family at Mount Ephraim practised her arias in the music room, in preparation for a performance that night at the Marlow Theatre in Canterbury. Soaring above the whine of chainsaws, her soprano voice provided an incongruously beautiful soundtrack to the scenes of widespread devastation outside: damaged buildings, acres of flattened orchards, wind-thrown branches, sodden leaves shrivelled and blackened by sea salt and the Victory, levelled and lifeless on the lawn, like a wrecked galleon on her side.

9

The English Channel

Thursday, 15 October–Friday, 16 October
Midnight

In the gathering howl of an English dawn,
a malevolent sea strips and throws its fossil bed
at the shifting shore

Rivers in the West Country were beginning to break their banks by early evening on Thursday, the fifteenth. Wind readings from Cornwall, Devon and all along the south coast were much higher than expected, and static caravans in coastal parks were folding and falling in their hundreds, but still the Meteorological Office's 9 p.m. forecast was for moderating winds, the shipping forecast for areas Dover, Wight, Portland and Plymouth relatively tame: 'South-westerly 6; occasionally gale 8 at first, becoming cyclonic 6 for a time, rain at times, moderate or poor.'

At 10.35 p.m., the Met Office revised its forecast and warnings of Storm Force 10 were issued for all Channel sea areas, but by the time these had been increased to 'Violent Storm Force 11 "imminent"' three hours later, at 1.35 a.m., the storm had already done what no one had expected. Instead of holding its predicted course along the Channel, it had twisted inland and although the vortex was over the Isle of Wight, its malevolent span now stretched from the Bristol Channel in the west, east as far as northern France and north towards East Anglia and the Humber Estuary.

By 2 a.m. the barometric pressure at Exeter was 957mb, the lowest recorded over England for 150 years but, even so, the full force of the storm had yet to be felt. It was between the hours of 2 a.m. and 5 a.m. on Friday, 16 October, that the storm intensified, particularly along its south-easterly flank, which included London and the south-east, the whole of the eastern Channel, the Dover Strait and the North Sea up as far as the Wash.

The 1.35 a.m. forecast arrived too late for ships at sea, whose crews had already experienced the strength of the wind: a Sealink ferry, the 5,590-ton *Hengist* moored at Folkestone, sustained £140,000 of serious damage to her hull when, in the early hours of the sixteenth, one by one, her twenty-four storm moorings popped and parted, forcing the captain to start her engines and put to sea. There were no passengers aboard, but the helpless crew were plunged into darkness when a colossal wave washed over her, damaging the electrical systems. Tidal streams off the breakwater, which are fierce even in normal conditions, carried the vessel east towards The Warren, a range of white cliffs with a sandy beach below.

The Warren is popular with fishermen, who bait their lines with herring strips, peeler crab and ragworm to fish for bass, cod, pollock and thick-lipped mullet off the rocks, or off one of the concrete aprons that slope out to sea. It was onto one of these groynes that the ferocious wind blew the *Hengist*, caving a hole in her hull ten by eight feet wide and grounding her on the sand. Her crew were rescued by breeches buoy when the worst of the wind had passed the following morning. After an operation to patch her up, which involved banking her high on the sand to get at the huge hole in her side, she was eventually refloated and towed back to Dover, stern first.

Another Sealink passenger ferry, *St Christopher*, which had left Calais in the early hours of the sixteenth, was forced to lie outside the Port of Dover in extreme weather conditions rather than attempt to dock and risk damage to herself or other vessels. The huge *St Nicholas*, on its way back to the UK from the Hook of Holland with hundreds of passengers, was obliged to do the same in monstrous waves outside Harwich Harbour. It was all the captains could do to keep a steer on their ships and ride the storm out till morning, engines running. Several untethered lorries on the *St Christopher* rolled about so heavily inside that their crashing impact over several hours damaged the huge steel doors of the upper deck, allowing water to pour in. Although the buckled doors would prove costly to repair, the physical damage was nothing compared to the exhausting experience of the eight hundred passengers trapped onboard the two ships, who finally stepped ashore at 2 p.m. the following day, having been forced to endure almost twelve hours of high seas and 100 m.p.h. gusts of wind.

Caught mid-sea, between the Hook of Holland and the port

at Great Yarmouth, a container ship, the *Duke of Yare*, her
cargo deck stacked to capacity, rolled dangerously in 100-foot
waves, her £6 million payload shifting with the ship as it veered
45° to port and the same to starboard. One by one, the giant
steel boxes slid from the open deck, like matchboxes, and
dropped heavily into the swell. At the port of Felixstowe, in
Suffolk, the hurricane-force winds set adrift a 1,300-ton tanker,
the *Silver Falcon*, sending her crashing into a jetty with her
lethal consignment of inflammable chemicals. The docks were
evacuated for fear of explosion, the ship saturated in fire-
retardant foam and the lifeboat called from its station at nearby
Harwich.

By 4.30 a.m. on Friday the sixteenth, the exhausted Hastings
fishermen had already left the beach and retired to the Angling
Club. At Mount Ephraim, the lucky fruit pickers were asleep
in the tea room, and in London, the Bloomsbury ambulance
crew had delivered the body of the homeless man from Lincoln's
Inn Fields to the mortuary at University College Hospital. But
in Harwich, the eastern harbour town that faces Felixstowe
across the confluence of the River Stour and the River Orwell,
the storm was only just reaching its terrifying peak.

10

Harwich, Essex

Friday, 16 October
5 a.m.

still we come
hungry
to say what has been unsaid
dying
to show what was made to disappear

At the old rail ferry terminal, overlooking Gas House Creek in
the port of Harwich, a solitary Sealink employee on the night
shift sat in his quayside cabin, windows lashed with rain,
watching in disbelief as the leaden sea rose and topped the
harbour walls. Violent gusts blew driverless cars into each other,
like dodgems, shoved barrels and crates against the tall metal
fences on the landing pier. Through the cloud, the man could
see the masted white shell of the old car ferry, the *Earl William*,
glowing in the rain-whipped dark and rocking ominously at
her moorings, a couple of yellow lights flickering in her small
square starboard windows. Tied to the dock by thirteen ropes
and with her engines stripped down, he knew the *Earl William*
wasn't going anywhere, but as the winds continued to strengthen,
he called the duty harbour master, the duty engineer and a
couple of his Sealink colleagues and told them, 'You'd better
get down here, fast.'

By 5.30 a.m., harbour officials and Sealink employees were
standing on the quay, holding on to each other for fear of being

blown into the water. The sea continued to menace the dock, the gusts intensified, and as they watched, in helpless, windswept amazement, the thirteen heavy ropes that held the *Earl William* to her berth snapped, one after another, their shredded traces whipping into the air.

On board the ship, which was now violently pitching and lurching, two seamen and a deck officer made frantic efforts to drop both anchors at the prow, but neither held. Harbour tugs and their crews mustered as the ship yawed from her mooring, crashed into a barge and a row of anchored yachts, then sailed drunkenly out to sea, ahead of the gale with a hole in her stern. The sturdy tugs sailed bravely alongside, but all attempts to rig an emergency tow failed and the dead ship[15] was blown uncontrollably across the harbour into the Stour towards the Shotley peninsula on the other side of the estuary, barely a mile from open sea.

Fortunately for all on board, after three hundred yards, the *Earl William* foundered on Trinity House moorings and, with a massive jolt, came to a trembling halt on a sandbank. Tug and harbour crews battled against the wind to steady and secure the enormous ship in case she made another wild bid for freedom.

By 7 a.m. the storm that had raged across the southern half of Britain, leaving a trail of devastation in its wake, had left Harwich, flying parallel to the coast, then thundering across the North Sea towards Norway, weakening rapidly. Within hours, the waters in the Stour estuary were flat calm and the skies were blue. Later, when the high tide lifted the *Earl William* off the sandbank, the tugboats were able to tow her and her uninjured charges back to port, with one of the onboard passengers, an experienced Egyptian sailor, at the helm. The ship arrived safely back at Parkeston Quay at 8 p.m. on Friday the sixteenth.

The *Earl William* was no ordinary car ferry, the Egyptian sea captain and the other passengers on board no standard holidaymakers either. Earlier that year, in May, the Home Office had commandeered all port facilities at Parkeston Quay and converted the old Sealink Channel Island ferry to a floating immigrant detention centre. It had stripped down her engines, reconfigured the lounges and cabins, sealed port-holes and replaced her maritime crew with security guards. On board, ninety-six asylum-seekers were awaiting decisions on their application to stay in the UK. The group included Somalis, Iraqis, Iranians, Seychellois, Afghanis, Ugandans and Nigerians, and a group of forty-six Sri Lankan Tamils, escaping brutal ethnic aggression in their own countries.

That port facilities, including Sealink employees, were now under government control was seen by many as welcome employment in a town that, in recent years, had watched the gradual decline of its fishing fleet, as well as the loss of the freight-boat service to the continent, but there was controversy too. The conversion of the *Earl William* from ferry to detention centre had prompted vociferous opposition in the House of Commons, with MPs comparing the ship to the notorious prison hulks of the eighteenth and nineteenth centuries.

But it was the Tamils' case that had attracted the public's attention. Earlier that year, on 13 February 1987, a group of sixty-four men, women and young children had arrived in Great Britain from the Sri Lankan capital, Colombo, via Malaysia. When they stepped off the plane at Heathrow and asked for asylum, they had believed that the UK, their former colonial ruler and a well-known champion of justice and human rights, would offer them shelter. They were, after all, in flight from a bloody civil war in Sri Lanka, a country racked with violence and intercommunal strife. To their dismay, they were refused entry and sent directly to Harmondsworth Detention Centre in west London, where they stayed for four days before being returned to the airport, for a flight back to Malaysia.

In protest at the court's decision, the men stripped to their underwear in Heathrow's departure lounge and, when forced to board, refused to fasten their seatbelts on the plane. They claimed that on arrival in Malaysia, the authorities would simply send them back to Sri Lanka and to certain death. Their dramatic actions bought them enough time for rapidly instructed immigration lawyers to obtain stay orders in the High Court, which meant that the government was obliged to allow the group to remain in the UK while their pleas for asylum were considered. The buses turned around. Some of the group stayed with relatives or sponsors; the rest were taken back to Harmondsworth.

In 1987, the tropical island of Sri Lanka, which hangs like a teardrop in the Indian Ocean off the southern edge of India, had been in a state of civil war for four years, after tensions between the Hindu Tamil minority – long-subjugated, disenfranchised, segregated – and the majority Buddhist Sinhalese boiled over. After centuries of being bounced between Portuguese, Dutch and finally British rule, independence for what was still Ceylon in 1948 came with a passionate sense of nationalistic pride for the Sinhalese, who continued to regard the immigrant Tamil population, many of whom had arrived from India as tea-pickers in the nineteenth century, with suspicion and barely disguised resentment.

In 1956, Sinhalese was declared the official language of the country, ignoring Tamil, spoken by 29 per cent of the population at that time, and in 1972, the country changed its name from Ceylon to Sri Lanka, antagonising the already defensive Tamil minority. In the groundswell of aggravated feeling, the LTTE, the Liberation Tigers of Tamil Eelam, was formed to call for a separate Tamil state.

Tamils began to leave the country in their thousands, as mob violence and fighting escalated, coming to a head in July 1983, when Tamil Tigers ambushed a military patrol in the north, killing thirteen Sinhalese soldiers. In Colombo on 24 July, angry Sinhalese mobs began to riot and, with the support of the police, the army and the government, killed four thousand Tamils and razing villages to the ground, raping the women and burning the men alive; children and old people were hacked to death, entire communities slaughtered without mercy. The events of 'Black July' propelled the country into full-scale civil war, which was to last another twenty-six years and leave more than a hundred thousand dead.

Life for the Tamil population, particularly young men, continued to be unsafe, particularly as the Sri Lankan authorities had begun rounding up all males between the ages of eight and forty, while on the other side, the Tigers were manipulating young Tamils and coercing them to join the rebel movement. Although most Tamils fled to America, Canada, Australia and South East Asia, many young Tamil men started travelling to the UK, usually in small groups of two and three. Then, in February 1987, the large group of Tamil men, women and children arrived at Heathrow.

In the 1980s, Margaret Thatcher's government was under increasing pressure to develop and implement a hard-line immigration strategy, but deciding who could stay and who to return to their own country was complicated. Under the terms of the 1951 Convention of Status of Refugees, migrants seeking asylum were asked to prove to British officials that they had a 'well-founded fear of persecution' in their home country, even though it was often impossible to prove whether asylum-seekers had suffered mistreatment or torture at the hands of their own governments. And if an individual could not actually *prove* that he or she would be personally targeted, was it right to send them back to a country where they would be conscripted to fight or, as was then happening to the Tamil population in Sri Lanka, if they were routinely persecuted and attacked in the streets? Some refugees arrived in the UK after spending time in other countries, but the British authorities clamped down on this too, saying they should have applied for asylum in the first country of arrival, rather than waiting to get to Britain.

On 24 February 1987, the day of the first High Court hearing, the group of Tamils were held under guard on buses at the airport, ready to board if the stay decision was rejected, but the Divisional Court found in their favour, opposed Mrs Thatcher and her home secretary, Douglas Hurd, and granted their lawyers leave to move for judicial review. The government took immediate revenge for the courts' decision, slapping penalties on airlines that knowingly carried passengers with inadequate documentation, announcing a revision of the asylum system and limiting the intervention of MPs in asylum cases.

The government then made a conscious effort to whip up public opinion against the Tamils: the minister of state to the Home Office, David Waddington, declared in Parliament that the Tamils' claims were 'manifestly bogus'[16], that the Tamils were 'criminals', even though medical evidence showed that some of the group were victims of torture. The following month, Conservative MP Terry Dicks stated that 'many thousands of people would be angered that these liars, cheats and queue-jumpers would be allowed to stay in the country';[17] other government spokespeople voiced concern about increased racism on the streets if too many 'coloured immigrants appeared'. All failed to ban the slogan 'White Britain First', so wilfully confusing the issue of asylum with immigration policy.

Humanitarian groups, refugee agencies and support groups feared that dangerous precedents were being set, but the

Thatcher government was impervious to criticism and refused to listen to their appeals or even to pleas for a less rigid stance from the Archbishop of Canterbury and the Chief Rabbi. The Tamils had found themselves in a country bubbling with anti-immigrant feeling and were at the mercy of government changes to migration policy.

In May, forty-six of them were transferred to the newly converted *Earl William*. The months passed, the government stalled. There were endless case reviews, but despite the tireless efforts of immigration lawyers, the legal status of the refugees remained unresolved. Refugee agencies, families and supporters of the Tamils and other nationalities aboard the *Earl William* complained that the asylum-seekers were suffering unimaginable distress and an unnecessarily protracted confinement; they claimed that the cabins were small, cramped and badly ventilated, that the port-holes were permanently sealed; that the food was inedible, the water undrinkable, medical attention inadequate and the women even denied sanitary towels.

Plans for the installation of a five-a-side football pitch, cricket nets and a volleyball court on the cavernous steel-floored car deck had never materialised; there were no separate facilities for prayer or for the nine women forced to share communal areas with the men, against their religious beliefs. By October, the government's inaction and the unacceptable conditions on board had already been the cause of two break-outs, a hunger strike, a 'lie-in' and a heavily publicised visit of support from young opposition back-bench MPs Jeremy Corbyn, Diane Abbott and Harry Cohen.

The violent displacement and release of the *Earl William* on the night of the Great Storm brought success for the Tamils where all human appeals for clemency had failed. After the events of the early hours of Friday, 16 October, the home secretary, Douglas Hurd, announced that on compassionate grounds, it would 'no longer be right to continue to detain those concerned on board the *Earl William*'. With no alternative accommodation available, the detainees were granted temporary admission to UK soil to stay with sponsors and relatives until their cases were determined.

There were still many legal hurdles ahead, but the Great Storm had brought the Tamils' long ordeal on the *Earl William* to an end.[18]

MPs visit Tamils held on prison ship

Three Labour MPs visited Tamil detainees aboard the prison ship Earl William at Harwich in Essex yesterday, where some have been on hunger strike for six days.

The Tamils, whose request for asylum has been refused and whose case is under judicial review, began the fast in protest against their detention.

Yesterday they withdrew "for the moment" a plea to go home to their families in Sri Lanka.

A group of 21 – nearly half the 49 Tamils who have refused to eat – told Miss Diane Abbott, Mr Harry Cohen (centre) and Mr Jeremy Corbyn that they were willing to go to Canada, France or Norway.

The Home Office said last night that none of the Tamils had asked to be sent home.

Mr Corbyn said afterwards: "We are concerned for the health of the Tamil refugees if they are forced to continue their hunger strike. One is already in a poor state, close to collapse."

Amnesty given, page 7

PART 3

THE AFTERMATH

11

Devastation

In the eye of a three hundred-year storm.

On the morning of Friday, 16 October, under a water-washed sky of mineral blue, the air emptied of birdsong, I stood, like millions of people across the country, ankle-deep in snapped twigs, slippery boughs and tawny wet leaves.

Overnight, the strongest gust in London was 94 m.p.h., the highest ever recorded in the capital, and on the coast at Dover, wind speed had been measured at a consistent 85 m.p.h. over a ten-minute period – the equivalent of a Hurricane Force 12, with 12 m.p.h. to spare.

More than fifteen million trees (the equivalent to 4 million cubic meters of timber) were uprooted across the south and south-east of the country[19], a quarter of a million trees in London alone. Cables and wires were brought down, leaving 150,000 households without telephone communication and hundreds of thousands of people without power for several days[20].

Eighteen people were killed in Britain, four in northern France. From Bath to Brighton and from Southampton to Southend-on-Sea, red phone boxes were upended and pavements uprooted by urban trees. Insurers across the country were inundated with claims for storm damage including those submitted by one in six households[21] in south-eastern England. The clean-up bill cost the UK insurance industry £1.4 billion.

British Rail suffered particularly badly: seventy-four trees fell onto a 2.5-mile stretch of line at Wadhurst in East Sussex; three hundred more along a thirty-mile stretch between Tonbridge and Hastings, the widespread disruption to services costing millions in lost fares. With bankers and traders unable to make their regular journeys into the City, the London Stock Exchange closed on Friday, the sixteenth, for the first time since 1974, exacerbating falling confidence in global financial markets, a situation that came to a head three days later in the stock-market crash of Black Monday.

Streets, parks and playgrounds, village greens and gardens were devastated, the estates and ancient woodlands of Surrey, Sussex and Kent destroyed. In the Pleasure Grounds of Petworth House in Sussex, designed by Capability Brown in the mid-eighteenth century, then painted by the artist J. M. W. Turner fifty years later, hundreds of years' worth of planting was destroyed in a couple of hours; 40 per cent of cricket-bat willow trees were lost in Essex, and at the prehistoric hill fort of Chanctonbury Ring on the South Downs, 75 per cent of the glorious beeches planted in 1760 by Charles Goring were uprooted by the wind.

After leaving the UK the storm moved across the North Sea, reaching the southern and western coasts of Norway on the evening of Friday 16 October. In Oslo, sea levels were the highest recorded for a century, causing severe flooding. Two million cubic meters (71 million cubic feet) of timber was lost, half of it in the heavily forested Hedmark region, and the country's insurance bill exceeded 500 million NKr (£45 million).

For several weeks there was a Dunkirk spirit, a combination of pragmatism, adrenalin and good humour, as roads were cleared, shattered windows replaced, crushed cars towed and power lines restored. In London, for a while, people gave up their seats for old men and pregnant women on the Tube and strangers chatted in animated groups on empty platforms and street corners. But if the urban drama was short-lived, the clearance of forests and ruined orchards, grand estates and conifer plantations had only just begun.

12

Moving On

the sweet,
too-short pulse
of your
honeycomb
heart

Since arriving in London, I'd had a variety of jobs: I'd been bottle-washer and waitress, yelled at from serving hatches by tyrannical chefs, taught English to Japanese school children in Kensington, delivered formal lunches to company directors in their windowless City dining rooms, and sat on the front desk of a recording studio in Baker Street (where, after failing to recognise Roger Daltrey one afternoon, I thought it might be time to move on).

I worked for months in that Italian deli in South End Green – where I learned to make a killer basil pesto, spent my days arranging handmade whorls of pasta on wire racks and came home every night smelling of Reblochon – until I found a job as a press assistant with the Royal Shakespeare Company at the Barbican Centre in east London. I worked late, attended previews and press nights, flattered actors in green rooms and dressing rooms, stood spellbound in the wings as rude mechanicals slept in enchanted forests, as kings, fools and men in kilts strutted upon the stage, and a sorcerer summoned a supernatural storm.

In December 1987, two months after the Great Storm, I was promoted. I left London and moved to Stratford-upon-Avon to work in the press office at the Royal Shakespeare Theatre, on the banks of the River Avon. I cultivated journalists, corralled photographers and cursed the critics. I sat in on rehearsals in vaulted rooms above the newly refurbished Swan Theatre and wandered the dimly-lit, plum-carpeted corridors during performances, standing at the back of the auditorium, watching famous actors in favourite scenes, mouthing their eloquent lines under my breath. In workshops and studios across town, I saw sword fights choreographed, crowns fitted and fabrics dyed. I watched costumiers sew buttons and beads on breeches, and silver clasps on cloaks and capes. I stood in awed silence as the company wigmaker teased individual black strands from a hank of real hair, harvested, she told me, from an Italian novice taking holy orders for the first time. I made new friends, formed crushes and unsuitable alliances, spent hours locked in at the Dirty Duck in the company of dressers, dancers, stage hands, spear-carriers and the occasional household name.

After a couple of years, I gave it all up to move back to London for a job at the Royal Court Theatre in Sloane Square, to sit in collaborative circles with charismatic directors, casting agents, literary managers and living, breathing playwrights. But in the end, I gave all that up too: to get married, have babies and go home.

My husband and I settled with our young family in a shabby old vicarage not far from my parents, in the perched Gloucestershire village of France Lynch, high on the wooded escarpment above the Chalford Valley near Stroud. Above us, gliders hung in silent span on upward columns of warm Cotswold air, while down below hidden trains hooted as they climbed the steep pitch to Sapperton Tunnel.

The house was built into the side of the hill. A high stone wall stood between the garden and a footpath that tipped down through brambled fields into Parish and Oldhills Wood.

In spring, the ancient beech forest was a tangle of walkways and elevated, sun-shafted paths trimmed with wild garlic and spurge laurel; in winter, after the leaves had fallen and before the deadening frosts arrived, the sound of the river in the valley drifted uphill and wound itself around the pale trunks like smoke.

For the first few years there, with three young children who couldn't walk far, or for long, we'd wander slowly along the flat canal path on the valley floor, or venture into the sloping barley fields in autumn, the children eating as many blackberries as they dropped into the wide plastic bowl. And every day I'd strap them into their car seats and drive the short miles down the hill and up the other side to see my father. I'd climb the steep stairs to his studio, always at least one child on my hip, to find him perched on his stool, painting in shafts of sunlight and drifts of smoke, every breath a battleground.

He loved the babies, held them high in the crook of his arm so they could run their fat, fascinated fingers over his eyes, his nose, his heavy moustache. If they were wakeful, the rhythmic wheeze of his chronically obstructed chest and the musty-old-cardigan smell of paint and nicotine was guaranteed to send them back to sleep.

Over time, as his health deteriorated, tubed staging posts were installed in the kitchen, sitting room, bedroom and studio, and oxygen was delivered to the house by Mr Allsop, a perspicacious, white-shirted white-van driver – and a closet narcoleptic. After struggling to the top of the house with the grey, recycled cylinders, Mr Allsop would pause on the landing to catch his convivial breath. As he talked about nodding off at the traffic lights or in the fast lane, my father would seize the confessional moment to snaffle an illicit cigarette, knowing that Mr Allsop, of all people, would never tell.

On a grey January day in 1998, after a family Christmas,

my father fell dangerously ill. I took the call, left the children at home and drove like a lunatic across the valley, to find my mother standing, like a shadow, on the doorstep, clutching his overnight bag in her hand, as the ambulance pulled away from the house. When it screeched to a halt in the middle of the lane, we just stood, the two of us, watching it, waiting for fifteen agonising minutes until the doctor opened the rear door of the van, stepped down and walked slowly back to the house. He shook his head, held my mother's hand and said how very sorry he was, but there was nothing more they could do.

My mother stayed alone in their handsome little house for as long as she could bear it, which was about a year, but she never went back up to his studio. It remained exactly as he had left it, that cold New Year's Day: a painting half finished on the drawing board, a jam-jar of pale pink water by the sink, a brush leaning against the rim, ash on every surface.

She moved once, then again soon after, the incrementally smaller houses forcing her to squeeze her treasured possessions into ever tighter spaces, piling boxes on top of wardrobes or under the bed, stacking cartons and crates in corners, arranging her extensive library of books three deep on every shelf. Paintings by my father that had previously hung alone were now grouped in incongruous clusters on every wall: a calm green Cotswold scene next to the sun-blasted streets of a Provençale town; a square-towered Norman church alongside the stilted fishing nets of the Gironde.

We joked about the clutter, but I knew exactly why she wanted to keep these things close. I understood how standing in the middle of a room, reaching out and touching your lost life with your fingertips might impart a small sense of acceptance and calm.

13
Finding Robert Games

GLOUCESTERSHIRE
September 2015

father whittled at my crib
pulling bark and heart shaped leaves
from slender yellow sticks of lime
bestowing on me nature's toys
freshly scented closely grained
smooth to my unseasoned grasp
brought me to the feel of wood
filled my head with forest songs

The photograph of the Kew Mural that I had discovered in my mother's spare room was now propped up against a pile of books on my desk, its contours, colours and contrasting timbers in direct sight, my father's dynamic design a delight and an insistent, beckoning finger. I was keen to track down the boy sculptor, Robert Games, if I could: I wanted to know more about his creative collaboration with my father and finding him was an important piece of the jigsaw.

I'd blithely assumed that he'd be a craftsman – a sculptor, perhaps, or a joiner, but to my surprise, after searching online, I found him working at a firm of patent attorneys in Cheltenham. I sent a polite introductory email, to which he responded with genuine modest surprise, suggesting we meet one day after work. So, on a warm, late-summer's evening, I left all my expectations behind and drove to his home in the Cotswold Hills.

We sat in the family kitchen, with its large windows and far-reaching countryside views, and talked easily for hours about the storm, about woodworking, about the Kew Mural and about our respective late fathers. Robert explained, with some regret, that with a busy job and two young daughters, he no longer had time for his old pastimes of wood sculpture and joinery, but he seemed happy to have the chance to discuss 'things past', as he put it, enthusiastically digging out old scrapbooks and a large black portfolio, crammed with photographs and newspaper cuttings.

In October 1987, Robert was sixteen and living in the small town of Llangynidr, between Brecon and Abergavenny, in South Wales, an only child and a boarder at the King's School, fifty miles away in Gloucester. His father, Gilbert, was an innovative and successful design engineer, but a man who found work 'a bit of an inconvenience, really' and whose true passions were for woodwork and photography. Eventually, Gilbert gave up his engineering job to run a small photography business with his wife from a studio in the Welsh valleys, which was only successful for as long as the proud mining communities of the Rhondda could afford to pay for their regular family portraits. The situation changed dramatically after the miners' strikes of 1984/5.

Nevertheless, working from home gave Gilbert the opportunity to pursue his hobbies and the chance to spend quality time in the school holidays with his son. His large purpose-built workshop was equipped with a band-saw, a lathe and its own kiln; planes, gouges, chisels and mallets, neatly arranged in descending order of size, were suspended from metal hooks above the bench. Gilbert built Robert a bench of his own and showed his son how to handle the equipment, which meant that the boy quickly acquired a level of skill far beyond that of his contemporaries, even of his teachers. Well-taught, enthusiastic and naturally talented, Robert regularly entered and won woodwork competitions, with his immaculately turned oak boxes, hand mirrors, drop-leaf tables and ladder-back chairs.

Inspired to experiment with unusual designs and new techniques, Robert told me, he and his father had subscribed to progressive American woodworking magazines. Together, they'd made a pair of huge Pennsylvanian sawbuck trestle tables in elm and oak and renovated an entire house from top to bottom, fitting new door frames and doors, joists and beams, flooring and staircases.

On the night of the storm, Robert was at home with his parents for the October half-term. South Wales experienced heavy rain and high winds that night, but escaped the structural damage and tree loss suffered on the other side of the country. Watching television reports the following day and shocked by the carnage at Kew Gardens, Robert wrote to the Gardens' director, the elegantly named Ghillean Prance,[22] outlining his idea for a commemorative storm sculpture.

With five hundred specimen trees down and another five hundred damaged beyond repair, garden staff at Kew had begun the long, heartbreaking task of clearing the debris: shredding small branches and sodden leaves, gathering broken boughs and ruptured stems, creating pyramids of timber all over the gardens, like sacrificial pyres. But Kew wasn't the only arboretum to have been damaged by the Great Storm.

At Wakehurst Place in Sussex, twenty-five thousand trees were lost and at Bedgebury Pinetum on the Kent/Sussex border, a quarter of the trees came down. At Ventnor Botanic Gardens on the Isle of Wight, where the storm landed with unexpected ferocity in the early hours of Friday, 16 October, many historic trees were lifted and tossed aside by the strong, salted winds (although the collection of palms, the oldest in the British Isles, survived).

Other significant collections of trees were affected too: fifty woods across the south-east owned and managed by the Woodland Trust were badly damaged, including Tyrrels Wood near Pulham Market in Norfolk and America Wood, an ancient pasture site near Shanklin on the Isle of Wight, where at least a fifth of the twenty-seven acres of woodland was demolished. At Stour Wood near Harwich, the south-east corner of the site was completely flattened, with thousands of mature oak and sweet-chestnut coppice lost, and at Ashenbank Wood in Kent, a Site of Special Scientific Interest (SSSI), expansive acres of oak, sweet chestnut, hornbeam and cherry were blown down.

In the Kent town of Sevenoaks, six of the seven mature Turkey oaks, planted in 1902 on the boundaries of the Vine cricket ground, were brought down by a particularly violent squall. Large areas of commercial woodland, valued more for their timber production than for their contribution to the landscape, were also seriously damaged, especially conifer plantations, which simply didn't have strong enough root systems to stand up to the extreme gusts. Although the loss of broadleaved trees was dominant, and 72 per cent of the damage occurred to privately owned woodlands and trees, the volume of commercial coniferous wood lost that night was equivalent to around five months of the UK's total timber production.

With 3.9 million cubic metres of timber from 15 million storm-damaged or fallen trees suddenly available, the timber market quickly became saturated and foresters were compelled to think creatively about its storage or disposal. In Suffolk, where pine forests were badly affected, the race was on to recover the wood before it was damaged by bark beetles and fungi, making it unsaleable. Four hundred thousand felled trees needed clearing at Rendlesham, three hundred thousand at Tunstall, and two hundred and sixty thousand at Dunwich; in all, 475,000 cubic metres, enough to fill 130 Olympic swimming-pools, the equivalent of thirteen years' wood supply.

In Thetford, Norfolk, a disused gravel pit was turned into a massive wet timber storage facility, drawing, for the first time in Britain, on the Scandinavian practice of preventing the development of fungal stain in conifer logs by water storage. Seventy thousand cubic metres of pine logs, freshly sawn from the roots, were stacked and sprinkled regularly with water, saving them from deterioration and allowing the markets to stabilise before the timber was released to be sold.

Kew had been inundated with requests for the exotic wood of their fallen trees. The directors recognised the demand and seized the opportunity to clear some of the excess timber, instructing garden staff to pile the mashed branches by the entrance to the Gardens, before opening the gates and allowing the public to take away whatever they wanted.

A few of the very rare specimens were reserved for three specific projects, marked out and approved by the Gardens' directors. Robert's mural was one of these, and he was in impressive company: his fellow craftsmen were the celebrated British furniture designer John Makepeace, and two lute-makers from south London, Stephen Barber and Sandi Harris.

'At the time of the storm,' John Makepeace told me, 'I was exhibiting in London and a television company was filming the exhibition. Knowing of my interest in forestry and woodland management, they asked if I would go to Kew the following morning to film the devastation there and talk about it for a news programme. It seemed important that the public should recognise the opportunity to give those trees an alternative future by commissioning furniture makers. I met with the Gardens' director and identified trees that should be saved from becoming firewood. Among those we selected were a walnut and a mulberry, which I said I would like, and I agreed to design a cabinet that would be displayed in a new building at Kew. In the event, the plans for the interior of the new building changed and the cabinet was no longer required.'

The furniture-makers who were asked to consider giving the trees that alternative future included Habitat and Ercol, but when the cost of recovering the wind-thrown wood proved exorbitant and their craftsmen were unable to guarantee the furniture's quality or stability, the manufacturers decided not to take the project any further.

Caption: The fallen trees identified and chosen in 1987 by John Makepeace have now been given that alternative future. Both the mulberry and the American walnut salvaged from Kew were used to make cabinets, while the mulberry was also used for an exquisite dining table in the shape of a leaf.

Gilbert hired a truck and drove with Robert, in eager antici-
pation, from South Wales to Kew. The scale of the recovery
operation in the Gardens was sobering: any excitement Robert
may have felt at the start of the long journey was soon tempered
by the sight of those freestanding woodpiles at the gates. No
Scandinavian-style stacking here: no pallets, crossbars or inten-
tional tilts, no careful eye for design, functionality or the look
of the thing. Shattered stems had been dragged or thrown onto
ragged heaps, the twist, stripes and circular patterns on the
sawn or split trunks darkened by heavy rain. Snapped-off
branches lay waiting for the chipper and smouldering bonfires
singed the air, the combustible tang of petrol jarring with the
sweet smell of sap and the earth-rip of ruptured roots. The
scene that greeted Robert and his father that morning was far
more shocking than anything they'd seen on television: this was
real, the comprehensive disfigurement of the Gardens laid bare.

Men in helmets, chaps, steel-toed boots and protective trousers,
working in surgical teams under skies the colour of stagnant
pools, barely noticed as Robert and his father walked through

the Gardens, studying the stacks of numbered and plated timber, selecting what they wanted and using their own chainsaw to cut the trunks into manageable lengths, filling the back of the van with walnut, larch, elm, lime, oak, beech, ash and pine, rare hornbeam, hickory and honey locust. The precious wood was taken straight to Sennybridge Sawmills in Usk to be planked, and from there to the drying kiln in their own workshop.

Several artists were then asked to present illustrative ideas for Robert's commemorative mural, but none succeeded in capturing the storm's drama, its energy or its destructive force. Eventually, Gilbert and Robert were introduced to my father through a mutual acquaintance – someone who had worked with Terry before, who knew his architectural illustrations, had read his book on set design[23] and who had seen the most recent of his large-scale paintings – a mural depicting *The History of Rugby*, commissioned by Twickenham, and hanging in the South Stand Rose Room at the west London rugby stadium at the time.

Hopeful that Terry would be their man, Gilbert called to make an appointment, drove with Robert from South Wales to the house high above the Woodchester valley and, as instructed, stood in the lane and shouted up to the open skylight.

Robert pulled an ink sketch from the folder. 'We visited your father several times to discuss the mural and he produced a series of illustrations like this for us.' He went on: 'As soon as I saw his drawings I knew I could work with them. I liked the fear in the faces of the lions, the powerful sense of movement Terry gave to the figures. I knew that I could translate those shapes, that power, into the finished work. In the end, after drying the wood and commissioning your dad, it wasn't until December 1988, more than a year after the storm, that I sent his final illustration to Kew, along with a wooden rabbit that I'd carved in the three-D sculpture effect I intended to use. They sent back a very nice letter telling me to take my time and not to allow the carving to affect my school work.'

He pulled a typed sheet of A4 from the folder, branded with the old Royal Botanic Gardens logo and scrawled with the flamboyant signature of a Dr Brinsley Burbidge, the then head of Information and Exhibitions at Kew. It read:

Dear Mr Games,

Kew's enthusiasm for your mural and our admiration for your skill are both almost boundless. I've shown the design and the photograph of the rabbit to a number of people, including the director, and received only delight at the way the whole project has now moved into a higher gear. I particularly like the image of our two lions defending Kew against the hurricane, which, as you say, is well portrayed as a running man.

It is very important that we find a suitable prominent site to display your work at Kew, and I will be discussing, with my colleagues, where best we can put a 9 ft x 5 ft mural. I have two possible sites in mind at present.

Please accept the best wishes from all of us at Kew for success in your open application to Cambridge and also our gratitude for your dedication to the Kew Project.

Yours sincerely . . .

If Robert's mother had known it would take her son more than a year to carve the mural, she might not have offered the family sitting room as a workshop. It took, by Robert's calculation, a thousand hours' work over a period of twelve months.

He explained the process to me: 'I projected Terry's illustration from a slide onto a large sheet of good-quality birch-based plywood and then I traced the shapes onto the wood with a marker pen. I carved the design in sections, using a thousand individual pieces of wood from thirty varieties of tree, completing the cameos – the rabbit, the urn, the lions, the life-size figure of the man – before attempting the background.'

And when the mural was finally completed, transported and erected it was unveiled by the Princess Royal, in a special ceremony to mark the opening of the new Victoria Gate Visitors' Centre in March 1989.

I drove home beneath an infinite apricot sky, swifts swooping and diving for insects in the cool evening air. I felt a personal sense of resolution: content to have solved the little mysteries that had surrounded the mural and delighted that Robert seemed to have enjoyed talking about it as much as I had. Perhaps both of us had felt our fathers with us in the room that evening; I know I had.

It had also been heartening to hear that Robert and my father had talked about a further collaboration: a second giant sculpture, which was to have been funded by the 1992 Garden Festival of Wales[24] and for which Robert had kept my father's preliminary designs and sketches. Although that project never did materialise, Robert received another commission from Kew four years later, for a much smaller wooden sculpture, to mark the royal opening of the new Jodrell Laboratory building in 1994.

Now I knew how it had all come to pass, how the wood had been sourced, dried, planked and shaped and how my father's design had been brought to life, I was determined to return to Kew and see the mural again, after all these years.

14

Royal Botanic Gardens, Kew

LONDON

October 2015

living treasures from flower rich provinces,
destined for the gardens of the western world

I stood at the Victoria Gate entrance to Kew Gardens, shivering. It had taken me ten damp minutes to walk from the Tube station, umbrella-less – as always, I'd come to the city unprepared. Even if I'd wanted to bring my country ways to the city, London had its head down in the rain. It would have been impossible to catch an eye and strike up a fleeting moment of soggy camaraderie with anyone on public transport. I told the man in the booth that I had an appointment to see the head of the Arboretum, Tony Kirkham, but that I was a little early. He nodded me through, so I pushed the turnstile and wandered over to the dry shelter of the Visitors' Centre to take a good look at the Kew Mural.

I moved towards it, instinctively lowering my face to the wooden surface, inhaling deeply. I ran my fingertips over the smoothly sanded contours, brushed the lions' hickory claws, their manes of yew, the limewood urn. I saw the skill and workmanship in the wind, five delicately spooned trumpets of palest ash, noted the exotic bird carved from fumed oak. In an instant, the smell transported me back to the kitchen of my Cornish grandparents' Falmouth home, where a pair of small sculpted heads, the size of a hand, mounted on little blocks, stood at either end of the mantelpiece: my father had carved these exquisite limewood portraits of himself and his sister, Joy, when he was still only a teenager. As a child, I'd always asked if I could hold them, tracing the soft relief with my fingers, curious to see my father's younger face, intoxicated by the warm, petrol smell of the shoe polish my grandfather used to treat the wood, buffing it afterwards to a warm glow with his handkerchief.

I stood back again from the mural and gazed at the thousand individually carved pieces of timber. Sunlight, air and the passage of time had taken their toll on its colours, textures and tones, but the detail and complexity of the design, the skill of the carving, were still clear to see. To me, the trees, animals and the iconic architectural features at Kew were a symbol of everything that had been damaged or lost that night across the southern half of the British Isles: the fragility of all our structures, the vulnerability of all our landscapes. Many years after that brutal, transformative event, the sculpture still managed to convey a sense of raw terror and shock.

A motorised green buggy pulled up at the kiosk, a bearded man at the wheel: Tony introduced himself and told me to jump aboard, then executed a sharp, one-handed turn. We trundled along the asphalt pathway at surprising speed until we reached what looked like a stable yard, where we parked. I hopped off the buggy and followed Tony through a draughty hallway, past an army of muddy boots and waterproof jackets on hooks, then up a short flight of stairs.

His office, warm and reassuringly untidy, had an elemental aroma grounded with base notes of creosote, like a garden shed; his desk, dominated by a huge computer screen, was piled with papers, the walls crammed with framed photographs and certificates. It might have looked and smelt like someone's bolt-hole at the bottom of the garden, but I knew

I was on hallowed ground. Kew is an international centre of botanical excellence, its labs, libraries and living plant collections among the largest and finest in the world, and Tony, as head of the Arboretum, is the hands-on head honcho, the weathered face of Kew Gardens, a charismatic Green Man who's had his herbaceous hands in the ground here since 1978.

Since meeting Robert and before arranging to see Tony, I'd requested access to Kew's considerable storm archive from 1987 and visited the Library Reading Room, housed in the modern Art and Archives section of Hunter House, a grade-II listed building just outside the Main Gate. The Kew library is a botanical treasure trove, containing several million books, illustrations, manuscripts and maps; Kew's world-famous Herbarium, an ever-growing collection of more than seven million dried and pressed plant specimens, as well as seventy thousand fleshy fruits and delicate flowers preserved in a liquid mixed to Kew's own recipe, is next door, in purpose-built, temperature-controlled units behind the original house.

In the Reading Room, I was presented with a collection of yellowing box files, containing hundreds of photographs and newspaper reports on the devastation at Kew, hand-written memos, multi-page documents, typed and held together with paperclips. I sat for long, silent hours at a sloping desk with my pencil, reading personal accounts from members of staff that described the night of the storm and its shocking aftermath. I read letters of sympathy from arboreta worldwide, offering seeds and replacement trees, studied estimates for the sale value of wind-thrown timber, graded lists and inventories of all the trees that had been damaged or lost. Some of these notes were written by hand, such as the one that listed the fallen trees in the West Arboretum:

ULMUS VILLOSA – a large specimen brought down, one of the few
  remaining elms which escaped the Dutch elm disease.

CATALPA COLLECTION – Badly affected with many trees uprooted
  and many more with broken limbs – this being due to the
  brittle nature of the wood.

UMBELLULARIA CALIFORNICA – Planted at the end of last
  century it was the only tree in the Arboretum.

MACLURA POMIFERA – The female tree of this species was
  brought down – rare tree from South and Central USA. Noted
  for its large compound trait.

Perhaps it was the inky scrawl, the way the handwriting slanted
on the page (a reminder that this happened before the widespread
use of computers); perhaps it was the easy use and musicality
of the Latin names or the way in which the individual characteristics of each tree were described with such familiarity that
moved me as I read it. The lists were genuine tributes to the
fallen, written by a human being in shock, with words and phrases
that echoed with a crushed sense of bereavement. It was clear
that, for all those who managed our parks and gardens, their
shock and grief at the storm's havoc and destruction were real.

Those who worked at Wakehurst Place, Kew's sister garden in
West Sussex, felt the same emotion, the same deep attachment
to trees and the same grief. An Elizabethan mansion set in 465
glorious acres, with steep, wooded valleys, ornamental gardens,
temperate woodlands and a sprawling nature reserve, Wakehurst
is beautifully positioned on rising ground on the western spur
of the High Weald, and was directly in the path of the storm's
100 m.p.h. winds. The mild, wet days before the storm had
turned the ground at Wakehurst to a glistening mulch; the brook
running to Westwood Lake in the south-west corner of the
estate was like a mill race; the trees, still in leaf, had only just

begun to take on the amber tones of autumn. In those few dark, turbulent hours, twenty-five thousand trees in Wakehurst's woods, wetland reserves and gardens were lost.

Staff had struggled through tree-blocked roads the following morning to find an estate depleted by the loss of 60 per cent of its entire collection: shelterbelts had been razed to the ground, precious ornamental trees had crashed to earth, narrowly avoiding the house, while mature trees that had withstood centuries of wind and weather had simply capsized, like sailboats on a lake. Familiar landscape features that had provided natural way-marking signs had all gone, including a handkerchief tree, *Davidia involucrata* – grown from seed collected in China in 1901 – a glorious rhododendron walk, two-hundred-year-old oaks, a swathe of trees planted in the mid-nineteenth century and an exposed pinetum on top of the hill, where resinous conifers, their shallow sandy roots slackened by rain, lay toppled in disarray, like spillikins on a table.

Years later, Andy Jackson, the director of Wakehurst, now retired, wrote that it had taken some time for the grief to pass. Staff who had worked in the gardens for more than twenty-five years, developing strong emotional connections to the trees, had witnessed their lifetime's work erased overnight and felt a profound sense of loss, akin to losing a family member or an old friend.

Tony scooped up a scrabble of papers from a chair by his desk and gestured for me to sit. 'I was in bed at home and was woken by the sound of a galvanised dustbin bumping down the garden path,' he said, settling into his own high-backed office chair and swivelling to face me. 'It must have been about two o'clock in the morning, but I went outside to rescue the dustbin because it was annoying me. I didn't realise how windy it was and I'd already lost a few tiles from the roof of my house.

I got back into bed and I remember saying to Sally, my wife, "It's a bit windy out there."'

Tony's a Lancashire lad, and straight away I warmed to the drift of his vowels, his gently understated turn of phrase. Brought up in the old cotton town of Darwen, he has lived in the south ever since he moved to Farnham in Surrey at the age of sixteen to take up an apprenticeship in forestry, but he's never lost the 'Derren' accent, his words still as soft as a Pennine stream over stone.

The following morning, despite London's Capital Radio advising people against unnecessary travel, Tony left for work as he always did. His usual fifteen-minute drive took him an hour and a half, through streets strewn with enormous city plane trees, their root boles standing more than ten feet in the air, the pavements around them lifted and distorted. He dodged, skirted and drove under fallen trees, all the time thinking, 'This is bad. This is major.'

Finding Kew Road blocked, he tried to approach the Gardens by a side street instead, but eventually gave up, parked the car and walked the rest of the way. Kew Green was like a war zone and blocked to traffic, with a row of uprooted horse-chestnuts on the ground. At Jodrell Gate, a colleague shouted over the wall to him from inside the Gardens, advising him not to go any further, but when he did, the scale of the loss was beyond belief.

He walked, disoriented, through grounds stripped of all the familiar arboreal markers, fought his way over piles of wet foliage to the columned and porticoed William IV Temple, where the main stem of a towering 150-year old Tree of Heaven, *Ailanthus altissima*, lay at a heavy angle across the recently restored roof, leaves clinging pathetically to its broken branches. He turned away, lost his bearings, tried to find the path back to the gates, but the way was blocked by more fallen trees, split trunks and shrubs unearthed. Where huge trees had fallen on their sides, gouging pits and craters in the sodden earth, the ground was like a moonscape, torn boughs and branches drooping in unwieldy piles of wet, green mulch.

With difficulty, he made his way towards the frame of the deconstructed Victorian Palm House.[25] The 19-metre-high glass and iron structure, considered by many to be the centrepiece of Kew, was undergoing essential restoration at that time: its 16,000 panes of glass had been removed, its resident tropical trees, cycads, palms and shrubs thankfully transported elsewhere for safe keeping. Tony clambered over the heaps of damp debris beside the lake, his heart heavy, and walked towards the Orangery, incongruously bright in this stark new landscape. Along the famous Broad Walk, five of sixteen American tulip trees, *Liriodendron tulipifera*, planted as an avenue in 1939, had been uprooted: tulip trees take between thirty and forty years to come to flower and the ones along the Broad Walk, of which Tony was particularly fond, had recently done so, in glorious mature profusion.

Almost one in ten of Kew's exotic trees had been lost in just a few short hours. The rhododendron dell and the bamboo garden were impassable, and the celebrated collection of hickories was damaged beyond repair. Some of the lost trees were rare, some old, others endangered, but all of them – even those with familiar names, like mulberry, maple or beech, poplar, lime, oak or chestnut – were of specific botanic or scientific interest and had been planted in carefully selected sites to allow them to grow into the shape and size that nature intended.

'Everything about that storm was unusual,' Tony told me. 'After a good growing season, but a very wet summer and a mild autumn, almost all the trees here were in big leaf and the earth was waterlogged. Under extreme pressure from a wind that blew from an unexpected direction and with no friction in the soil, the rootballs simply rotated in the ground and let go.'

A *Quercus bicolor*, a swamp white oak from the forests of the eastern and central United States, the biggest of its kind in the UK, lay beached on the wet grass and the *Ulmus villosa*, a huge and endangered Marn elm from the slopes of the Himalayas, a scientifically important tree that had survived Dutch elm disease, had been torn from the ground, like a weed. An English walnut, *Juglans regia*, planted by the Queen in 1959 to mark the two hundredth anniversary of the Gardens, and a Japanese cedar, *Cryptomeria japonica*, planted by Emperor Hirohito of Japan on a state visit in 1971, had both succumbed. The oldest of the fallen trees were a sweet chestnut, believed to have been at least three hundred years old, a Lebanese wild apple, *Malus trilobata*, one of the best specimens in cultivation anywhere, a Turkey oak, *Quercus cerris*, which had stood by the Palm House Pond, and an ancient Iranian elm, *Zelkova carpinifolia*, planted by the Gardens' founder, Princess Augusta, in 1761.

The ravaged Gardens were closed to the public and every tree examined. Had it rocked? Had it lifted? Was it safe? The scale of the task ahead was daunting. Kew relies on income through the gates, so the priority was to clear up the mess and make some areas safe enough for the public to visit again, which they managed after only twelve days, although large parts of the Gardens remained closed for months.

With so many mature trees upended, Tony and his colleagues at Kew and Wakehurst had the chance to study the long-buried root systems of their fallen giants; it was a once-in-a-lifetime opportunity, although not one they'd asked for. At the same time, the government statutory body, the Countryside Commission,[26] set up Task Force Trees, a plan to 'make good the damage caused to amenity trees and woodlands, in towns and in the countryside, and to lay the foundations for a 10-year programme of recovery'. 'During the 50 years before the storm,' their action pack declared, 'the south-east lost 40 per cent of its deciduous woods – and hardly anybody noticed. After the storm, millions of people woke up to the value of trees in the landscape of both town and countryside.'

Two questionnaires, designed and processed by scientists from the Jodrell Laboratory at Kew,[27] were distributed to landowners and interested members of the wider public, to gather as much information as possible about the trees that had succumbed.[28] At Kew, Wakehurst Place and other wooded sites across the south-east, hundreds of storm-damaged trees were photographed, their height, crown and trunk diameters recorded, their root systems analysed and growth rings examined. Trunk and root material was collected, stored, dried, frozen, ground and screened. The results showed that the trees with the highest 'incidence of blow' included *Quercus* (oak), *Fagus* (beech), *Pinus* (pine), *Picea* (spruce) and *Betula* (birch), while those least likely to fall were *Aesculus* (horse-chestnut), *Prunus* (fruit trees, such as plum, cherry and peach), *Salix* (willow) and *Alnus* (alder).

At Wakehurst, where shallow soil covers sandstone rock and many trees appear to be shallow-rooted, they have, in fact, a deceptively durable anchor, their roots able to penetrate deeply into rock fissures, but overall, sandy soils proved the least tenacious, while wet clay and loam gave trees a much stronger grip.

Many tall trees were lost: the average height of all fallen trees measured was 18 metres, a sad indication of the vulnerability of trees in their prime, but some species, such as native oak trees, with their strong roots, and the *Sequoiadendron giganteum* (giant redwood) at Wakehurst remained remarkably resolute and upright.

Most trees fell in the direction of the prevailing wind, unless there were buildings to obstruct them or the land was shaped in such a way as to cause the wind to eddy. In London, and in other towns and cities, many trees fell into the road, which implied that the buildings had deflected the wind, allowing it to strike from a direction against which the trees had developed little root strength. And in forests and on plantations, once the trees on the perimeter were down, those sheltering within, with their reduced root strength, stood little chance of survival, leading, in so many cases, to complete devastation.

Tony pulled a scrap of paper from a drawer and drew on it with a pencil. 'Think of a tree like a wine glass,' he said. 'The crown of the tree is like the goblet, the stem of the glass is the trunk and the flat base is the root plate. When the tree is at its heaviest and in full leaf, as most still were in October 1987, the spread of the root plate, like the wide base of the glass, is what stops the tree falling over.'

In arboreta, trees have often been transported and transplanted and some specimens may have failed to develop a strong taproot, which would have left them vulnerable. Most of the upturned trees revealed well-developed lateral root systems, but the average depth was surprisingly shallow, most measuring between 0.5 and 1.5 metres. In addition, some trees had been planted too close together, resulting in poor root systems, tall, spindly growth and an unnaturally high centre of gravity.

There was evidence to suggest that the old-fashioned planting technique of dropping a young tree into a round hole filled with rich compost meant some of the older trees had failed to develop that necessary, wide-spreading anchor. 'For if a tree has no need to stretch out and find its own food,' Tony told me, 'the roots stay within the planting pit, becoming "pot-bound", a bit like a plant you might buy from a garden centre that's been sitting around on the stand for too long.' He continued: 'The storm changed everything. We now dig shallow, square pits with no added organic matter so that roots are forced into the corners to seek out their own food and grow as widely and as quickly as possible, which establishes the tree and builds crucial *independence*. These techniques encourage root systems that are stronger, more stable and better able to hold the tree upright in a storm.'

I suggest that if the storm had led to such a dramatic change in working practices in the way trees are planted and managed, then perhaps it wasn't such a bad thing, after all. 'It was a wake-up call,' he said, with feeling. 'You can't ever avoid storms, but we learned a hell of a lot from the 1987 storm, and everything we do here now is in preparation for the next one.'

And as gardeners and woodland managers in other parts of the country mopped up and cleared away the debris, frantically planting huge numbers of new trees to try to restore the land-scape to its former self, behind the gates at Kew, arboretum staff were beginning to see things differently. They saw that the storm had done, overnight, what no landscape gardener would have dared to do, namely, to clear the arboretum of the oldest and most decrepit trees, the ones that should have been felled, but hadn't been, which in turn allowed for new planting and much-needed rejuvenation. Where at first they had seen only loss and devastation, they began to see opportunity and regeneration, realising that what remained was more important than that which had been lost.

At Wakehurst, the apparently indiscriminate sweep of the wind had left ground staff, including one of the junior gardeners, Iain Parkinson, reeling. Iain is now Wakehurst's Conservation and Woodlands Manager, but in 1987, aged only twenty, he had just swapped his deskbound City job for permanently dirty fingernails and a life outside on his knees in all weathers. He knew little, then, of the botanic value of the collection, but was seduced by Wakehurst's wild beauty and eager to learn from the older gardeners, men who still wore a jacket and tie to work, who handed him and the other aproned juniors their wages in brown-paper envelopes on Friday afternoons.

With Wakehurst's landscape transformed overnight, Iain watched as the estate was subjected to a radical clear-up. Huge fires were built in the pits of upturned root plates, some burning for months, as more and more debris was cleared. Stumps and roots, trunks and branches were piled into old quarry sites around the estate, deep craters full of decomposing wood that still, to this day, steam on cold winter mornings. As at Kew, the urge to return the land to normal, to restore order and allow the public to return, was strong. But in doing so, heavy plant-clearing machinery compacted the earth, the soil was disrupted, some areas became waterlogged and trees that had survived the storm began to suffer from stress and succumb to disease.

In some parts of the estate, though, in Tilgate, Wakehurst

and Chiddingly Woods, nature was left to recover without intervention, and a different woodland structure began to emerge. As the canopy changed, so did the availability of light to the forest floor; nutrients locked up in fallen trees were fed back into the soil as the trees decayed; rare mosses, ferns and lichens were given free rein and huge numbers of woodland birds returned to nest and breed.

Tony jumped up and told me to grab my coat. I followed him downstairs, climbed back onto the buggy, holding tightly onto my seat as we rumbled away from the office building. Tony drove one-handed, gesturing with the other as he explained where we were going and why. We followed the pathway towards the Victoria Gate, skirted the south side of the lake, and the Woodland Garden, ending up at the north end of the Princess of Wales Conservatory, stopping at the site of the Turner's oak, *Quercus x turneri*, one of the oldest trees at Kew, planted during the reign of King George III.

Before the storm, this tree (a cross between an English oak and a holm oak, created in 1783 by a Mr Turner, a horticultural innovator from Essex) was in very poor health, with a thinning crown and small leaves, dead wood and suckers all along the main trunk. As the flailing gusts reached their peak on the night of the storm, Mr Turner's oak was lifted, like a plug, out of the ground, but instead of falling over, it dropped back into its pit and settled again, remaining upright despite its severely shaken roots. The following morning, beleaguered staff, who had a thousand other trees to deal with, left the old oak, assuming it had suffered too much to survive and expecting it to have breathed its last. Several months later, when they returned to the tree, they were surprised to find it in rude health. It's still standing today, and in the years since the storm has put on another 25 per cent of its canopy.

This was natural disturbance in action: the violence of the wind had done the old tree a favour, it seemed. Its lift and resettlement during the storm had allowed air to circulate around the roots, de-compacting the bole, rejuvenating the hard, lifeless soil that had been pounded by lawn mowers and thousands of feet over the last 250 years, allowing oxygen to reach its complex underground life-support system.

Amazed by the exponential growth and rejuvenation of the Turner, Tony and his colleagues identified other mature trees in the arboretum thought to be suffering from similar compaction and tried to mimic the storm's disturbance, to see if they could get the same results and bring a few of the old-timers back to life.

The old trees were treated to a large dose of nitrogen gas, delivered through a probe injected into the soil around the base of the tree, shattering the compacted soil, creating open fissures, improving the exchange of gases and allowing water to percolate more evenly throughout the soil. Then, a second injection into the roots: a cocktail of mycorrhizal fungi and bio-stimulant. Finally, the base of the tree was covered with shredded wood, leaves and horse manure to feed the mycorrhizae and to act as a cushion, preventing re-compaction. The dying trees rallied, the improvement was spectacular. The results were so remarkable that the aeration and mulching process for mature trees was adopted at Kew and in other arboreta all over the world.

Back in the warmth of the office, Tony described to me how he and his colleagues walked the ravaged gardens in the wake of the storm, assessing what they would need to do to restore the collections to their former glory, aware that it would take them many years to achieve. Wherever possible, shoots and seeds that had been salvaged from the fallen trees were preserved in cold stores over the winter, ready for propagation the following spring; botanic gardens the world over, including New York, the Arnold Arboretum in Boston, Kirstenbosch in Cape Town, Hawaii and Chicago, offered replacement trees and, over the course of the following year, some of the storm-blown spaces in the arboretum were filled with trees from the Gardens' own nurseries.

But there were still gaps at Kew and at Wakehurst that couldn't be filled. Both taxonomically and geographically, there were areas of the world, particularly the temperate woodlands of the globe, which were no longer represented: South Korea, Japan, China and Taiwan, which were no longer represented. Some species had survived but others had gone for good. The only solution was to return to the countries in question and collect the plants at source. The golden age of plant hunting had long passed, but the storm had opened a new and necessary channel of exploration and enquiry.

A consortium of scientists and horticulturalists from Kew and a variety of other botanical institutions made a series of expeditions to China and eastern Asia, the first in the year immediately after the storm, targeting specific areas, especially Sichuan, taking with them a list of plants that had been lost and a wish list of many others. The following year, Tony and a colleague from Wakehurst Place, the horticulturalist Mark Flanagan, flew to South Korea for the first of many field trips and seed-collecting expeditions they would make together.

Tony stood in front of his crammed bookshelf, pulled down a large glossy hardback with his own and Mark's names in white capitals along the spine[29] and handed it to me, asking if I knew anything about Ernest Wilson, the Edwardian plant hunter. I grimaced and shook my head, anxious that my ignorance might offend, but Tony seemed delighted to introduce me to the man he described as his hero and 'the leading plant hunter of his generation'.

With genuine awe and admiration, he spoke of the young horticultural student from Kew who'd wandered the inhospitable and unexplored regions of China and the Far East for a decade between 1899 and 1910, doing the same in Japan, Korea and Taiwan in subsequent years, sourcing, collecting, preserving and transporting woody plants, flowering species, hardy trees and shrubs to the UK and to the United States. Wilson's legacy to Western horticulture, Tony told me, was the introduction of over a thousand species, more than any other collector, many of them new discoveries to science and some, such as *Magnolia wilsonii*, *Cordyalis wilsonii* and *Iris wilsonii*, that have taken his name[30].

The significance of Ernest Wilson's achievements became even more apparent as Tony and Mark covered thousands of Far-Eastern miles of their own, on their series of seed-collecting expeditions in the years after the storm. Time and again, they found themselves walking in Wilson's footsteps, whether in the wooded valleys of South Korea, on the peak of Jum-bong in the Diamond Mountains or in the hills above the small fishing port of Dodong, on the volcanic island of Ulleung-do. After climbing Taiwan's highest mountain, Yushan, rising through alpine forests and beyond the tree line to marvel at the same breathtaking 360-degree view afforded to Wilson in 1918, their appreciation of the hardships and challenges he had faced in his tireless search for new botanical specimens made their admiration for him even greater.

At Wakehurst now, the landscape is moving into a new cycle. 'It's sometimes hard to remember the sight that greeted our staff on that blue-sky morning after the storm,' Iain Parkinson told me. 'Today's restored landscape is the result of a balance between the active management of the formal gardens and exotic plant collections, whilst allowing the more holistic process of natural regeneration to take place in the woodlands. One of the downsides to the increased light levels, however, has been an increase in alien invasive species, such as *Rhododendron ponticum*,[31] and a proactive approach to controlling its spread through the woodlands has been necessary. But, thirty years on, it's rewarding to see that our restoration methods have worked and that Wakehurst once again showcases formal gardens and internationally important plant collections within the context of the wider High Weald landscape.'

And, thanks to the storm, Kew is now a young arboretum. In 1987 it was old, supporting far too many aged specimens, but with judicious planning and planting, trees that were propagated from fallen specimens are now growing well, others gathered on expeditions are flourishing and the collection is already moving into the next age span.

At both sites, the storm's disruption proved a catalyst for change, providing opportunities to reinvigorate and develop the collections and shift the botanical emphasis from empire to education. As Wakehurst's former director, Andy Jackson, put it, 'An arboretum used to be a playground for the rich to show off their acquisitions. Nowadays, we are part of an international community that is doing its best to mitigate species extinction, and educate and inform the public.'[32]

I walked back through the Gardens to the Museum, where items from Kew's Economic Botany Collection were on display in the long-running 'Plants and People' exhibition.[33] I was hoping to find the six-course lute that had been crafted using exotic timber from fallen trees after the storm and which, like the mural, was one of the three special projects to which Kew had given its official blessing.

I soon found it, with its amber-tinted belly, glowing under lights in a glass case and displayed alongside other musical instruments that had been made using different types of plant: a pair of rubber drumsticks, some ebony castanets, a rosewood flute. The lute was much smaller than I had imagined and an object of exquisite craftsmanship and staggering beauty: its neck, pegbox and fingerboard came from a fallen pagoda tree, its back ribs from wind-thrown Osage orange.

Immediately drawn to discover more, I called the luthiers, Stephen Barber and Sandi Harris, explained my interest in the storm and asked if there was any chance that I might come and meet them. To my delight, they invited me to visit them at their south London workshop the following day.

15

Peacock Yard

breathed his passion,
shaped my own

Peacock Yard is a pink and grey cobblestone mews flanked by two-storey workshops at the centre of the Pullen Estate, in Kennington. It's an area of tall, yellow-stoned, late-Victorian artisans' dwellings, that stands in utopian architectural contrast to the grim post-war housing that surrounds it. A century ago, cooperatives of bookbinders and printers, makers of clogs, hats, brushes and ships' fans occupied these flat-roofed buildings, their wide stable doorways edged with blue brick quoins. Still functional, the workshops now house artisans for a different era: silversmiths and ceramicists, architects, publishers, photographers and luthiers – highly skilled creators of beautiful stringed instruments.

A van turned into the yard and parked. A blonde woman and a bearded man in a peaked cap waved and beckoned me towards the door, all smiles. I followed them up a narrow stairway to the dark workshop where Steve unfolded a couple of old director's chairs and Sandi put the kettle on, flipped a switch on a giant Anglepoise lamp and sat on a stool at a raked drawing table, in a clouded pool of lemon light.

Hanging on the wall, in uneven vertical threads, were about fifty lute shells, some ridged, some smooth, all highly polished, their deep, rotund bellies like giant pear drops. On every available surface, hundreds of un-labelled jam-jars in regimented piles, four high and twenty deep, each one shimmering with twists of silvered metal or filled with mysterious clips, catches, plugs, pins or pegs.

'The sheer volume of fallen trees in London parks and the subsequent collapse in the timber market meant that borough councils all over the capital were inundated with unwanted wood,' said Steve. In the chaotic weeks after the storm, he and Sandi had driven around the city with their own chainsaw, harvesting the broken boughs and enormous trunks that were still lying on the ground, many of them already stripped of their leaves, making identification difficult. Wearing a protective helmet, glasses and gloves, Steve sliced through fallen plum, pear and walnut, mature apple and flowering cherry, breaking broad lengths of Hungarian ash, lime, poplar and yew into manageable-sized logs with a heavy-duty chainmill. On Clapham Common, in south London, they recovered a huge, figured maple, whose crisp white hardwood has long been the instrument maker's wood of choice. All this, as overwhelmed parks officials simply stood and watched, saying, 'If you can move it, son, you can have it.'

A tabby cat slid from behind a sheet of ply and picked her way towards me on her *pointes*. She arched her back, stretched her front, leaped onto my lap, and began to knead, insinuating her sharp talons into my flesh, opal-eyed, ecstatic. (Uncanny how cats always seek out the person who likes them least.) I looked up to where short-necked lutes, in seasoned shades of amber and burnished brown, dangled from every rafter; to where pale, unfinished guitar bodies and other, less-familiar, wooden shapes were slung from door jambs and lintels. Behind me was a dense wall of timber, like a horizontal forest; planks and shafts in a variety of widths and colours, stacked on top of each other in unmarked piles all the way to the ceiling. I could only assume that some kind of sensual filing system of smell, texture and grain was in operation, for none of the wood was stamped, tagged or identified in any other way.

Steve moved towards a large metal cage under the window, slid back the bolt and casually released an enormous grey rabbit, which lolloped over the threshold and sloughed silently under the worktops. Sandi, now modelling an alarming full-face head torch with built-in magnifiers, gouged wood in curls, like apple peel, from a flat piece of spruce, pushing the chisel's short, concave blade into the fine white timber around a decorative template.

We talked about the types of wood used for different parts of the lute: the soundboard, the body, the neck and fingerboards. 'We use bone, not ivory, for nuts, end buttons and finials,' said Sandi, looking up, her eyes like saucers behind the giant lens, her voice strangely amplified, 'and for our neck veneers and fingerboards, we have a supply of old satinwood that we inherited from Stephen's grandfather, who was a master cabinet-maker.' 'One of four brothers,' added Steve, 'artisans all, my grandfather the only one of them to survive the Great War.'

They explained that they try to use timber and other materials that are as close as possible to those used by the great sixteenth-century luthier Laux Maler – 'the Strad of the lute world', Steve called him. For their lute backs, they, like Maler, prefer to use Hungarian ash (*Fraxinus excelsior*), for its delicate markings and for the crisp, clear sound it makes. For their soundboards, they use a variety of seasoned spruce, collected at source from the forests of Bavaria, which has a rippling pattern in the dense grain and produces even tones, right across the range.

Steve explained that the selection of wood is the most important factor in instrument making, as the type of wood used can either inhibit or favour vibrations, depending on its individual characteristics. 'The stringed instruments made by the Italian luthier Antonio Stradivari have long been the benchmark of excellence for violin-and cello-makers,' he told me, 'and it's the density of the wood he used to make them that gives them their superior tone and brilliance.'

Stradivari, born in Cremona in 1644, used wood from spruce and other trees harvested during a seventy-year climactic period of reduced 'sunspot activity', known as the Maunder Minimum. Sunspots are areas of reduced surface temperature on the outer shell of the sun that are linked to a variation in the solar magnetic field. They vary in size and diameter, and appear at different times, depending on the eleven-year solar cycle. Between 1645 and 1715, a diligent English astronomer, Edward Walter Maunder, had noted that as the sun became bigger, slower and colder, only forty sunspots were observed, compared to the usual forty thousand.[34]

When dendrochronologists examined the narrow rings in trees that grew during this period, they confirmed the slowest arboreal growth rates for five hundred years, and discovered that the wood from these trees was significantly denser than that of trees that had grown faster under normal climatic conditions.

'Stradivari also used other techniques and methods that set his instruments apart,' added Sandi. 'He treated the wood with fluorides, chrome and iron salts to prevent woodworm; he applied two layers of varnish, the first oil-based, the second mixed to a special recipe that included oil, pine resin, pigments and pure phlogiston, which was said to be gathered from a secret location, under a full moon, in the foothills of the Piedmont mountains. But it's thought that his use of dense wood affected by climatic cooling over many decades is what gives his instruments their exceptional acoustic quality.'[35]

Steve and Sandi insisted that neither of them plays the instruments they make to any recognised level, yet they seemed to have a natural understanding of sound, tone, temperament and pitch. What other qualities does a luthier need? I asked.

'An ability to think laterally,' said Sandi, 'and a love of problem-solving, both of which I appear to have inherited from my father. He was a commercial artist, a model-maker and a medievalist, who built weapons and armour for battle re-enactments in his spare time.'

Steve, too, spoke of the skills handed down to him by his own father, 'a musician, though an engineer by trade' and of the special recipe for fish glue mixed with gin bequeathed to him by his grandfather, the art-deco cabinet-maker, a man who'd immersed himself in the complexity of geometric design to bury those painful memories of the trenches and of his three lost brothers.

I thought of Gilbert Games and of the gifts he'd passed on to his son, Robert – the precision, the passion, the fine crafts-manship – and recognised the same legacy of creative perfection in the Barber's lutes: the thirteen-course baroque model in birds-eye maple, striped with plum; the ten-course lute with a pear drop-shaped shell, carved from the unusually figured Holbein maple; the one with a deeply fluted back, made from the wood of the jujube tree, with a cypress-wood heel and internal slipper block. All of them hand-built, from scratch, to authentic medieval designs, in this dimly lit workshop with its wild-eyed cat and its resident lop-eared rabbit.

Four months after the storm, Steve had received a call from Kew Gardens, inviting him to recover some of the specimen trees that were still lying in the arboretum: a giant 130-year-old Osage orange, a rare Californian laurel – known as the headache tree for its pungent leaves, which smell like bay – and a fine brown-timbered pagoda tree, with which he and Sandi went on to make a series of pitch-perfect, six-course, early Renaissance lutes, one of which I'd seen in the Museum the previous day.

These trees may have come to a violent and premature end,

but in their sanding, shaping and sounding, the recovered timbers had revealed unique acoustic and structural qualities that had granted them the same 'alternative future' as the wood in Robert's mural, and the mulberry in John Makepeace's exquisite leaf-shaped table.

When it was time for me to leave, Sandi pushed her headset onto the top of her head and raised her chisel in farewell. Steve accompanied me down the stairs, past the bulbous lute bodies and out into the sunshine, to where an overgrown honeysuckle bush grew unwieldy next to the loading bay. As he pushed back the branches and disturbed the foliage, I was hit by an intense bosky smell and squinted beneath the greenery to see a waist-high pile of dark orange logs.

'We still have plenty of wind-thrown Osage left,' he told me, 'enough for at least another thirty years.'

I made my way back to Paddington, arrived back in Stroud and drove home from the station. I needed fresh air and some thinking time, so I swapped my London skirt and city shoes for jeans and an old jumper, pulled on a pair of wellingtons and took the dog for a walk in Standish Woods. I followed the Cotswold Edge through towering stands of veteran beech, all the way to the windy heights of Haresfield Beacon: the Severn, a splinter of light on the horizon, the towers of both bridges into Wales caught in surreal shafts of cloud shine.

I knew that if I was ever going to understand how 15 million trees were lost in one night, and how, almost thirty years on, the landscape had recovered, I would need to widen my research. I'd need to talk to ecologists and conservationists, to anyone who could help me think above and beyond the tree line and guide me to a deeper understanding of the complex relationship between humans and the natural world.

As I walked, I made a mental list of the people and agencies I could approach.

I reflected on all I'd learned so far: how fascinated I'd been by Tony Kirkham's description of trees as family members; intrigued that in forests, trees live like humans do, in mutually reliant communities, supporting each other, as well as a web of biodiversity that includes mosses, ferns and fungi, birds, mammals and insects. I was enchanted by the idea of mycorrhizae, the underground fungal network, through which trees and plants communicate and share resources.

'In the redwood state parks in California', he'd told me, 'there's a rare albino redwood with ghostly white needles instead of the usual green ones. These mutants grow to barely a fifth of the height of a normal hundred-metre redwood and, because they are unable to make chlorophyll themselves, they take sustenance from the surrounding family unit, sheltering in the shadow of other redwoods, surviving only by tapping into the root structures of neighbouring sequoias, usually the parent tree from which they sprouted in the first place.'

The mural had inspired me to take the first steps on this journey of discovery, and I wondered where my sometimes-wayward spirit of enquiry would lead me next. I must have scuffed those wide, leaf-littered trails through Standish Woods a hundred times, the dog trotting and snuffling ahead of me, but now, I found myself looking at the familiar trees with new eyes. I could almost hear the forest babble beneath my feet, the arboreal conversations above my head.

16

What is a Wood?

GLOUCESTERSHIRE
February 2016

spurge laurel, bluebells and buckram
drink streaks of sunlight
in this blessed beech cathedral

I find David Russell in an unassuming cottage that backs windowless onto a Cotswold lane, its foundations sunk into the hillside, its frontage tilted over a hidden valley of uneven fields and sloping beech woods. We sit in a book-lined study, the air still and scholarly, like inked parchment, the vertiginous valley view silently framed by wide windows and velvet drapes, the half-hour sounded by the chime of a grandfather clock in the corner. A black lurcher ties her flat-coated frame into a bony bow next to me on the sofa, and a friendly, thin-skinned whippet sinks onto a cushion at David's feet; he covers her tenderly with an old blanket and pours me a coffee.

'I'd only been in the job for a year when the Great Storm tipped everything on its head,' David tells me. 'Like everyone else, I was shocked by the scale of the devastation, intent on recovery and fired up by good intentions.'

Having heard first-hand about the post-storm revitalisation of arboreta at Kew and Wakehurst, and in my quest to discover how the wider landscape had recovered after the storm, I'd approached the National Trust, many of whose large and historic estates across the south and south-east had been seriously damaged that night. Ray Hawes, the Trust's genial head of forestry, had not only offered invaluable insights into the Trust's conservation practices, and inspired me to plan a trip to the grand houses of Surrey, Sussex and Kent, but he'd also introduced me to David, his old friend and his predecessor at the Trust: the man who'd been in the hot seat in October 1987. David and his teams had worked around the clock overseeing the efforts of regional managers as they tidied up the mess and replanted storm-damaged woodlands across the south and south-east.

'A few months into the clear-up', David continues, 'meteorologists presented us with a new and persuasive theory. They said that the last time a storm had hit the UK with such ferocity was in 1703, but that there was clear historical and meteorological evidence to suggest that catastrophic storms of this magnitude occur every two to three hundred years, with a twenty-to twenty-five-year period of less destructive, but nonetheless violent storms also known to crop up at the end of each century.'

David pulls a hand over his Gandalfian grey beard. 'This information drove a jump in thinking: ecologists could now say, with confidence, that great storms, though catastrophic and upsetting, are not *imposed* on nature, they're *part* of it, that they occur within the natural course of events and are part of a naturally changing and unstable environment.'

The dog lying beneath the blanket snores. The clock chimes. Thoughtfully, David continues: 'There was a tendency to think of the storm as a damaging event, but when you know that your woodlands are going to blow over every two hundred years, that they are always in the process of recovering from the last great storm, when you know that they are composed the way they are and look the way they do precisely because of the destructive effects of that storm, then you begin to *relax* in the knowledge that woods are just being woods and doing what woods do.'

His words, carefully chosen and softly spoken, hang in the air. Silence follows and, for once, I resist my wittering urge to fill it. I'd heard the phrase 'natural regeneration' for the first time only a few months earlier, but had been studying it closely since then. I now knew that the unprecedented violence of the storm had generated exceptional horizontal as well as vertical vigour in our woodlands: as trees fell and canopies changed, new light had brought new life to the forest floor. I also knew that storm-damaged woods across the southeast had been overwhelmed by natural regeneration as seeds, blown by the wind, had taken root in systematically cleared woodlands in and among the rows of newly planted trees in blue plastic tubes.

'I should tell you,' David says, changing his tone, 'that although I'm a forester by training, and although I worked for the Trust for sixteen great years, I no longer work in forestry. You see, I never really was a forester, in my heart. I'm more of a romantic. I've always thought of woods as places of transformation.'

My mind makes an immediate associative leap to the enchanted forests of myth and folklore, to Robin Hood's greenwood, the Brothers Grimm and the 'green plot' of *A Midsummer Night's Dream*, with its cast of fickle fairies, its magical combination of disorder and fantasy. David seems to be reading my mind. 'A rational approach to nature can only take man so far,' he explains. 'There's a role for the non-rational in conservation too. Woods are *places* and should be recognised and celebrated as much for their cultural, social and aesthetic significance – which includes their associations with fairy tale and legend – as for their practical and economic value.'

In 1987, David already believed that working with the flow of natural change was preferable to trying to control it. After the storm, supported by illustrious like-minded colleagues, such as the academic Oliver Rackham, the woodland ecologist George Peterken and Tony Whitbread, the chief executive of the Sussex Wildlife Trust, he began to promote the idea that, rather than racing to clear a damaged site, humans should stand back from the chaos of a wind-thrown wood while Nature was at her most dynamic: trust her to heal herself in time, to lie on the ground, to rot, self-seed and grow.

Although I acknowledged the storm for the traumatic event it undoubtedly was, I'd stopped thinking of weather as a malevolent force and found the suggestion that I should *relax* and allow Nature to reset her own dials both appealing and reassuring. Perhaps that makes me a romantic too. I suggest that perhaps the storm wasn't such a bad thing after all.

'It was neither good nor bad,' David replies, with a smile. 'It was just natural and Nature tends to be unconcerned with morality.'

There's a loud knock at the door. The lurcher rolls off the sofa, and bounces towards the kitchen, barking. David follows. The whippet's tiny head, with its beadlike eyes, pokes momentarily from beneath the blanket, then retrenches.

I take a moment to sit back and look around the room: floor-to-ceiling oak shelving obscures a long wall, every slot and space crammed with books; under the window a leather-topped desk is covered with papers, files, magazines and more books – novels, non-fiction, collections of poetry, philosophy texts, ecology, photography. There's no doubt that David's personal relationship with the natural world is intellectual: I wondered how he'd managed to reconcile such a strong romantic instinct with the pressing practical demands of his job during such a challenging time.

He returns to the study, the prancing lurcher at his heels, a chewed slipper in her mouth. I pat the sofa and she jumps up again and lies gazing at me with adoring eyes, her front paws and muzzle on my knee.

When I'd first spoken to Ray Hawes, an affable, fast-talking and busy forester with a mere 8.5 million trees on National Trust land to oversee, he'd explained that, back in 1987, the management of a woodland was adjusted depending on what was required from it. For the National Trust and other agencies, such as the Woodland Trust, this has always meant balancing conservation, land management and forestry with safe public access. But for commercial foresters, many of whom managed forests on behalf of pension funds at the time, it was all about using the land as a resource, squeezing as much as possible out of a plantation for profit.

In 1987, there were already tensions between commercial foresters and environmental organisations about the level of human interference in our woodlands. After the storm those tensions would heighten further. The natural recovery advocated by David and other ecological experts required patience and a high tolerance of disorder while the landscape readjusted, but neither of these qualities was in great supply in the immediate aftermath of the storm. Land owners, foresters and woodland managers were facing extensive clearance problems and huge bills.

'And anyway,' David explains, 'the clearing and replanting were an essential part of the healing process. There was a powerful and emotional sense of ownership among communities and managers who loved their woods and needed to *do* something. What we were asking people to do was to wait and see, but wait and see is not very human.'

David tells me how he has long found inspiration and guidance in the work of the American conservationist, forester and philosopher Aldo Leopold, whose book *A Sand County Almanac,* written in 1949, influenced the development of the early environmental and rewilding movements. Leopold rejected society's sense of ownership over the land and offered a definition of conservation as a 'state of harmony between men and land'. (His observations on wolves as predators that introduced the concept of trophic cascades – when predators suppress or alter the behaviour of their prey, releasing them from predation – have also become a central tenet of rewilding.) He stands up, goes to his bookshelf, tilts and extracts a well-thumbed paperback, then flitters the pages until he finds the short passage that sums up his own attitude to conservation. He reads it to me:

'I have read many definitions of what is a conservationist, and written not a few myself. I suspect the best one is written not with a pen but with an axe. It's a matter of what a man thinks about while chopping or while deciding what to chop. A conservationist is one who is humbly aware that with each stroke he is writing his signature on the face of his land. Signatures of course differ whether written with axe or pen, and this is as it should be.'[36]

Another thoughtful pause: 'I wanted to develop this element of mindful woodland management,' he tells me, 'question our long-held ideas about nature, conservation and landscape and ask how, in the aftermath of a three-hundred-year storm, we should manage and conserve our woods for the future.'

David devised a workshop for land managers and staff, called it *What Is a Wood?* and asked participants to take their working hats off and think about what woods meant to them *personally*, not what they thought they *ought* to mean to the National Trust. He asked where we get our ideas about how Nature ought to look. To what degree have science, history and aesthetics shaped our thinking? What are the other important demands on our environment – food, timber, recreation, biodiversity and wildlife?

And how was it received? I wonder. David smiles. 'Not everyone appreciated my unconventional approach,' he admits. 'The intention was to move traditional forestry and land management towards a less invasive wardening system, and instead of asking, "What do we do?" I wanted to ask, "What happens if we do nothing?" to encourage a shift in perspective, ask which woodland sites needed managing and which could, realistically, be left alone. Most foresters are sensitive to the complexities in woodland systems, but this intervention of mine was nevertheless interpreted by some as unsupportive and as a dilution of their professional function and responsibility.'

And thirty years on, I ask, is woodland management more *mindful* than it used to be?

'I'm probably not the one to ask,' he replies, 'having been out of the way of forest management for so long, but my suspicion is that, as in so many other spheres of endeavour, conservation managers are much more outcome-oriented and unwilling to risk uncontrolled change. In a world of corporate accountability, there is much less encouragement for a manager to write "his signature on the face of his land".'

It's time to take the dogs for a walk in the woods. We fetch jackets, hats and gloves, pull boots on, clip the shivering whippet into a waterproof coat and set off up the hill under an ironstone sky, heads down against a bitter wind.

I am persuaded, absolutely, that less is more; that there can be real gains by allowing instinct and emotion to guide decisions about the landscape; that man and Nature rely on each other for survival and that only a respect for this mutual dependence will ensure the survival of the planet. But, of course, I benefit from living in the countryside without having to make any of the big decisions about its management. I recognise that the real challenge for the agencies, landowners and foresters who act as guardians to our green spaces is the careful management of change: adapting conservation practices within a constantly changing natural environment and working in the interests of both nature and man.

And, as we trudge uphill, the dogs pulling earnestly on their leads, I find myself wondering whether these post-storm pleas to accommodate nature's processes may have inspired, even helped to frame, more recent ecological initiatives, such as Wild Ennerdale (a valley in the Lake District, jointly managed by the National Trust, the Forestry Commission and United Utilities, where nature is being given the freedom to shape the landscape) and the rewilding movement, whose declared aims are nothing less than the mass restoration of ecosystems, particularly in the treeless uplands, and the re-establishment of missing species, such as beaver, boar and lynx, in the wild.

We take a footpath that follows a high ridge through the wood: it's wide, muddy and deeply rutted with fat tyre marks, and lined with recently felled beeches, the sawn blond stumps glistening, raw and rough around the edges, the severed trunks on the ground, split into casual lengths. The forest floor is tawny with fallen beech leaves; strands of grey winter light drop into the slender leafless gaps between pale, perpendicular stems.

This woodland was planted for timber in the 1890s, with larch and imported European beech seedlings, although there have been quarries, pasture and woodland here since Saxon times. There were once beech, ash and oak plantations all over the country, when wood was in huge human demand: we farmed it to build our ocean-going ships, to make our roof beams and joists, using it for house frames, flooring and fuel. Over time, as new building materials displaced timber and coal replaced wood as an industrial and domestic energy source, coppiced woods and plantations, less frequently harvested, gradually turned into woodlands, just like this one.

And when woodlands like this one blew over in 1987, people blamed the perceived uniformity of age and species for the exponential loss of trees, although David assures me that we lost trees of all ages and of all different kinds that night. Certainly, thousands of beech trees were lost from exposed sites, but so were oak, ash and birch, chestnut and hazel, millions of conifers and hundreds of exotic species from gardens and arboreta. Many younger trees fell that should have stood, while older trees, rotten hulks with hollow trunks and no crown, defied the wildness of the wind and stayed upright.

The composition of our woodlands changed too: birch and sycamore, thought by many to be undesirable colonisers, rushed to fill windblown gaps where graceful beeches had once stood. 'That some beech woods may never be dominated by beech again is not further evidence of the storm's destruction,' David tells me, 'but merely nature's latest *alteration* and part of a continual process of evolution and change to which we will all adapt.' He goes on, 'It's not a good idea to get too fixated on the diverse structure of woodlands. After all, whatever regrows in the aftermath of a great storm is natural. What's not natural is clearing it all away.'

I've learned that for a wood to be truly natural, there needs to be a lot more deadwood on the forest floor than is currently left to lie in British woodlands. Man has traditionally used wood for his own needs, harvesting and removing trees while

they are still young. By contrast, in the vast, primeval
Białowieża Forest in Poland, 50 per cent of the trees are either
dead or dying and left to rot on the ground, a percentage ten
times greater than in our managed forests (and upon which
twelve thousand living species are said to depend). Here, on
our small, populous island, with its paucity of woodland,[37]
deadwood is uncommon, because almost all our woods need
to be managed to some degree, and it's unusual for trees to
lie untouched or for the untidy process of natural regeneration
to dominate. An oak tree, for example, is traditionally harvested
at a hundred years old whereas, in fact, oak can live for five
hundred years and, if allowed to lie, can take another fifty to
a hundred years to rot down and return to the soil.

I'd spoken to the conservationist, Tony Whitbread, who had
told me about The Mens, a large area of woodland in the Low
Weald, managed by the Sussex Wildlife Trust. Here the storm
damage of 1987 was so great that the decision was taken not
to clear it but to let it recover naturally. In time, the huge holes
that had been blown in the canopy allowed sunlight to reach
the forest floor where saplings and new trees have now grown;
unusual fungi and insects feed on the rotting timber of the
fallen trees, and ancient woodland trees, like midland hawthorn,
wild service and spindle, have now sprouted in secluded glades.
Where once beech and oak trees were equally dominant, oak
is beginning to take the lead. 'Barely managed, and with a
primitive, untamed atmosphere,' Tony told me, 'The Mens is
as near to an ancient wildwood as can be found anywhere on
this island.'

The dogs run ahead. We scuff the soft, wide paths in a sloping
circuit until we reach the road again and I walk, waving, towards
my car in one direction as the dogs pull David home in the
other. I sit for a moment with my thoughts, conscious that I

feel richer for this conversation; braver, too, as if instinct and intuition have been given a voice.

I think back to my country childhood, remembering how absorbed I'd been in my outdoor life. Steeped in the sounds and smells of the stall and the open field, I'd moved subliminally through my early years and intuitively into my teens, always knowing that I was happiest outdoors, simply sucking up the fresh air. And although I've never tried to express my relationship with the natural world in words before, it feels as if that's beginning to change.

I was seven when we moved to Gloucestershire from North Wales. At the village school, a farmer's daughter befriended me, inviting me to spend weekends with her on the family farm, which I continued to do for the next four formative years.

Together we clung to a metal bench under the old Land Rover's flapping canvas as it jarred and jumped tracks over dusty, yellow fields, carrying ice-cold drinks to haymakers on hot days. On winter mornings, when herds of dark-eyed cows stood still as tombstones in frosted fields, their breath like shot straws of smoke in the Arctic air, we halved hay bales, and pushed the scented segments from the back of a moving trailer, the tractor's tyres forging swerving patterns on the ice-whitened grass.

Her father, the farmer, taught me to ride, *heels down, heart up*, on sluggish ponies in a pair of cast-off jodhpurs and a soft-peaked, hard hat of worn brown velvet. I grew to love the stable smell of straw and fresh manure, the soapy feel of leather in the tack room, joyfully adding the words 'numnah', 'snaffle' and 'Pelham' to my vocabulary. On Sunday afternoons, when it was time to go home, I remember finding short-cuts down the hill through badger runs, back lanes and bridle paths, and in the garden, I balanced broom handles on baked-bean tins, forcing the dog to canter over them, satchel straps wound bridle-like around his long-suffering shoulders.

I held a severed fox's paw in my curved palm when my friend returned blooded from her first hunt. I witnessed a piebald foal slide from its mother at dawn in an open field, then watched the dazed mare eat the purple-streaked afterbirth where it lay on wet grass, like white unmoulded jelly. One sleepover Saturday, after a day spent calving in the fields with her father, my friend, newly enlightened, told me the truth about what happens when a bull mounts a cow and, by impli-cation, what our parents got up to in their bedrooms. On mattresses in the ambrosial attic, where cooking apples lay in rows on the creaking floor, we spent the night giggling in horror and realisation, our torchlight on the bulging walls as distorted as the strange new world we now inhabited.

I had no idea then that these vital, visceral childhood episodes were a rural initiation that would benchmark my future exist-ence, set me apart from my parents and siblings. Looking back, I suppose nature just *happened* to me, on Sunday-morning rides, trailing the others, dreaming, on a sofa-backed pony, my friend constantly turning in her saddle to point things out, and make sure I was keeping up.

We rode out in all seasons, and what I learned, I learned in cycles: that spring was here when hawthorn bloomed, like confetti, in the hedgerows, when the mistle thrush bounced across the fields, when cuckoo chicks begged their loudest. In still summer air flecked with smithers of hay dust, I lay on my back, squinting at an unbroken blue sky, sucking ice cubes or blowing hollow grass between my thumbs. I caught wasps in jars of sugared water, found blackbirds' nests in hedges and sticklebacks in shallow streams, learned to distinguish an ashling from an oakling, knew where to find the fattest blackberries, when to collect the finest acorns, the shiniest conkers. In the early autumn, I stole windblown apples from a neighbour's garden, noticing that the trees changed colour when the air was spiced with woodsmoke and the evenings began to draw in.

I start the car and drive slowly home. Perhaps I have always known that the way to live within the landscape is to walk alongside it, treat it with wonder and compassion.

PART 4

THE ROAD TRIP

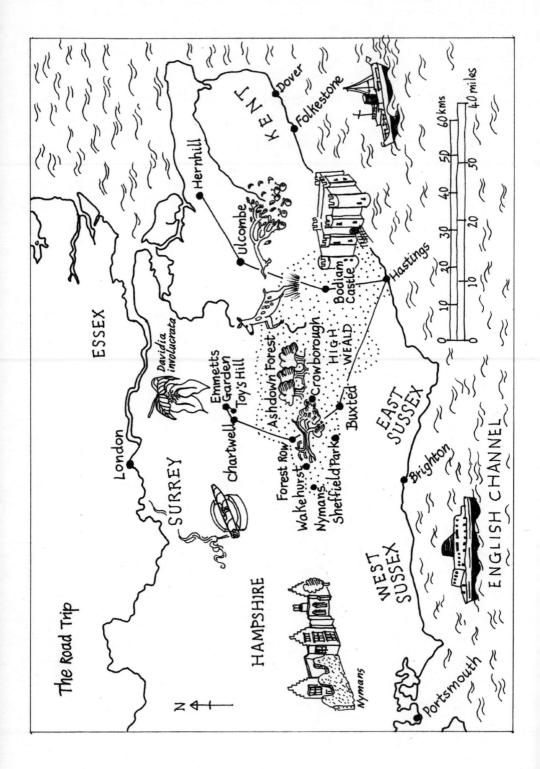

The Road Trip

17

Ashdown Forest

SPRING
2016

on sloping stands defenceless ashlings grant a glimpse of sky
and tawny beech woods fill and fall beneath me like a sigh

Thin curtains filtered the first light of dawn, throwing a pale blue tint across the pulpy walls. Awake and already alert in the unfamiliar surroundings, on a single mattress on the floor under an open window, I lay and watched the curtains lift and drop with the shallow morning breeze, heard distant cockcrow and the first strains of spring's celestial soundtrack.

I rolled off the mattress and onto the carpet, lifted an old satin-edged blanket from the back of a chair, draped it around my shoulders and stood at the window, hugged in mauve. The faded red brick of the tumbledown cottage was green-stained with moss and lichens, and an uninhibited 'Albertine' threw its spiny, copper-pink-tipped shafts at the flaking sill. As I watched the sun rise, the air filled with the perfectly pitched chorus of early worm eaters: gallant blackbirds, robins and thrushes, a wren, pushing its sweet song skyward, and the wandering voice of the male cuckoo.

I was in the village of Forest Row in the acoustic heart of Ashdown Forest, ten square miles of ancient heath and woodland in the High Weald of Kent, an area devastated by the storm nearly thirty years before. Straddling the four counties of Kent, Sussex, Surrey and Hampshire, the Weald is the fertile

Neptunian remains of what was once a deep ocean sea, between the parallel chalk horizons of the North and South Downs. The High Weald lies between them, on top of a giant geological up-thrust, a gorgeous green sandstone dome, exposed and eroded over millennia.

My hosts in this budget B-and-B were an exuberant, wild-haired, trilingual Dutchman called Piet, his Japanese wife, Mitsuko, and their two dark, beautiful, barefoot boys. The house was small and chilly, and all of us seemed to be sharing the same tiny bathroom on the ground floor, but it was cheap and clean, and the welcome had been warm when I'd arrived on their doorstep, late the night before.

I'd decided to start my 'storm road trip' in Ashdown Forest after talking to Ray Hawes, whose own startling storm experience had taken place here. In 1987, recently married and working as a commercial forester in Surrey, Ray had just moved with his wife to a house in Crowborough, a small town on the edge of the Forest. As the winds increased in strength in the early hours of Friday, 16 October, he sat bolt upright in bed, mesmerised by the demented sway of a 70-foot oak tree in his garden, never thinking that the worst would happen. But, like a scene in a disaster movie, the thrashing tree that was lurching back and forth loomed menacingly towards him one last time, then just kept on coming, crashing through the window of his bedroom and landing within three feet of him and his wife.

When we met, it was clear that Ray's terrifying ordeal had had no effect on his enthusiasm: he's still as passionate about trees as he is pragmatic about their conservation, though I sensed that for him, as for everyone I'd met so far, the Great Storm remains one of the most significant and transformative events of his professional life.

Ray had suggested that I visit Toys Hill in Kent and I'd spent the day there, guided around the most comprehensively storm-damaged woodland in the entire south-east by Chris, a National Trust ranger. Two hundred acres of high woodland to the south of the North Downs, with far-reaching views across the Weald to Ashdown Forest, Toys Hill was one of the first areas of land gifted to the National Trust by its founder, Octavia Hill, in 1898. But its magnificent hilltop setting was also its downfall on the night of the storm as, in just a few brutal hours, 98 per cent of its mature tree canopy, largely beech and oak, was lifted off and blown away.

The bulldozers were brought in and the site cleared, new trees sourced and the woodland replanted. In time, however, the newly planted trees were overwhelmed by vigorous natural regeneration and forced to compete for light and space with birch and sycamore saplings, and other trees that had sprouted naturally from windblown seeds. The wood had quickly become dense and impenetrable. Wildlife and biodiversity had suffered.

By contrast, in neighbouring Scords Wood, an experimental area of non-intervention, wind-thrown trees were left to lie where they had fallen and, over time, plants such as bilberry and clematis, honeysuckle and heather, unseen in the area for more than a century, began to grow again on the open ground. Woodlarks and nightjars, birds that had been scarce in that part of Kent for decades, returned to live and breed, and wildlife thrived in the post-storm landscape.

From Toys Hill, we'd walked to neighbouring Emmetts Garden, an elegant Edwardian house and six-acre estate, also managed by the National Trust. The garden at Emmetts, laid out in the nineteenth century by the owner Frederic Lubbock, was designed with the help of his friend, the innovative Irish horticulturalist and writer William Robinson, its borders packed with exotic and rare trees and shrubs from across the world. Influenced by the Arts and Crafts movement, Robinson promoted individuality and natural development in his designs, encouraged shape, colour, growing habits and foliage, rather than adherence to a strict layout, and favoured permanent rather than bedding plants, as well as a mix of native and exotic shrubs and bulbs.

But the 1987 storm had no respect for historical design, style or content, carelessly flattening the whole of the surrounding woodland and a host of priceless specimens, including an Atlantic cedar, a Judas tree and a tulip tree. Spectacular aerial shots taken in the immediate aftermath show the carnage. Since then, however, the garden at Emmetts has been extensively and sympathetically replanted: its rock garden and lily pond have been preserved, the integrity of its formal rose garden restored, and in springtime, the bluebell displays in the replenished woodlands are more dazzling now than ever before.

One of the reasons I'd wanted to visit Emmetts was to see the handkerchief tree, *Davidia involucrata*, for the first time. During the storm, a particularly violent gust had blown the beautiful flowering Chinese specimen in the South Garden to a 45-degree angle, but as almost half of its roots remained in the ground, garden staff had decided to winch it upright and keep it there.

To my delight, I found the tree on a sheltered slope behind the house: at the end of its flowering season, the grass around its base was scattered with fallen white petals, each fading bloom curling and brown at its oval edge. A few ghostly double bracts still hung in the branches above me and, although past its best, just the sight of it, a tree so lovely, so unique and once so prized, was a source of almost idiotic joy. I knew just how far its nutmeg-shaped seed, collected by Tony Kirkham's horticultural hero, Ernest Wilson in 1901, had travelled from south-eastern China all the way to an Englishman's garden a hundred years ago.

I'd then wandered around the gardens at Winston Churchill's

former home, Chartwell, where the 'heavenly tree-crowned hill', described by his wife Clementine on her first visit to the house, and the sweeping parkland that featured in so many photographs of the great man, had been levelled by the storm. His grandson, the young Winston Churchill MP, said he was thankful his grandfather was no longer around 'to witness the scenes of devastation in the valley that he loved so much and which he and my Grandmother made their family home for more than forty years of their lives – he would have been inconsolable.'

It had taken the National Trust more than two years just to clear the park and high woodland at Chartwell of the debris but, to me, the regenerated estate looked as green and vigorous as I imagined it might have looked before the storm, those iconic views from the house and the formal gardens, so adored by Churchill, restored.

I'd visited a cluster of parks, palaces, mansions, woodlands and leafy estates in the same area, many in the guardianship of the National Trust, almost all of which had been damaged as the storm passed through in the early hours of 16 October and left reeling from the vicious sting in its ferocious tail. At every site, after dogged clearance, propagation and replanting, thirty years of regrowth has now camouflaged the original damage. I still had striking photographic evidence,[38] though, to remind me of just how heartbreaking the destruction had been at Chiddingstone Castle, north of Tunbridge Wells, at Hever Castle, the childhood home of Anne Boleyn, and at Standen House, in West Sussex.

The park and gardens at Sheffield Park on the banks of the River Ouse in East Sussex lost more than two thousand of its trees and shrubs that night, but with a new drainage system and a vibrant mixture of new plants – four thousand trees and shrubs, including acers, rhododendrons, azaleas and 150

English oaks, ingeniously planted among the veteran storm survivors, the park has been returned to new glory. At Nymans, home to the creative Messel family since 1890, a property that had already suffered a catastrophic fire in 1947, 80 per cent of the trees fell, including a historic collection of rare pines, a giant monkey puzzle and twenty so-called 'champion' trees.

Harold Macmillan's house at Birch Grove, in West Sussex, and Hughendon Manor, Benjamin Disraeli's home in the Chiltern Hills, were badly hit. At Scotney, the small, romantic medieval castle near Tunbridge Wells, where Margaret Thatcher once had a flat, the estate took the full blast of the storm, losing 183 of its 531 trees, including a Cedar of Lebanon, a rare and mature wild service tree and eight out of thirteen limes, the oldest of which, at 293 years, had fallen heavily into the moat. Leaving nature to her own devices in formal gardens such as these had never been an option. Thirty years on, after careful clearance, patient propagation from trees on site, extensive planting programmes and thousands of new trees, these signifi-cant estates have now been restored.

Of the 15 million trees felled by the Great Storm,[39] 12 million were in forests, the rest in parks and on estates like Chartwell; 360,000 trees were lost on National Trust land alone. Trust employees who had access to traumatised sites in the storm's immediate aftermath said that in some places they could walk on fallen trees for three or four miles in one direction without their feet ever touching the earth.

There was a human cost too: rangers and wardens, some of whom had worked for more than twenty years caring for beloved gardens and woodlands, cracked up and stepped down, unable to see how the landscape to which they had devoted their working lives could ever recover. Such emotional attachment to the land and to the trees that grew upon it made me think of the grieving staff at Wakehurst Place, only twenty miles south-west of Chartwell, and how that glowing green corner of the country, so close to London yet so rich in gracious open parkland, had borne the full cruel brunt of the storm.

Two weeks after the storm, the Trust launched an appeal, with the Prince of Wales as Patron, and was soon overwhelmed with donations. Members of the public responded with emotion and huge generosity, galvanised by drastic television images of the flattened forests and apocalyptic acres of devastation. Margaret Thatcher is said to have contributed specific trees to the appeal for Chartwell's restoration. Suddenly more aware than ever before of their landscape, more appreciative of the trees around them and alarmed by what had been lost, people made it clear that they wanted their parks and woodlands back, whatever it took.

This strong sense of propriety, coupled with grief and inten-sified by shock and panic, drove the first wave of post-storm activity: bulldozers were brought in, rides and woodland were cleared of damaged trunks, split boughs, branches and piles of leaves; even the soil was scraped away. Some of the smaller woodlands were levelled completely, leaving only the occasional beleaguered crown of a survivor tree in a sea of cleansed and disturbed soil. Trees were logged and stacked in regimented piles, but unless the wood could be rapidly and economically stored, it was unceremoniously burned in monumental bonfires.

Across the storm-damaged area, tree surgeons, contractors and the military were called in to help with the clear-up: chain-saws, already responsible for up to thirty-six thousand injuries each year, caused thousands more when hundreds of enthusi-astic but untrained operators got their hands on the potentially lethal equipment. Countless new trees were planted in the cleared ground: row upon row of nursery seedlings in plastic sleeves, many imported to satisfy the enormous demand. The media promoted the message that our woodlands had been neglected, that most of the trees that had succumbed were old anyway, and that a replanting regime was needed to reinvigorate our landscape.

I smelt coffee and sock-footed it down the narrow staircase into the kitchen where Mitsuko gestured to me to join her boys, who were sitting up at the table in full pirate gear, working their way through ceramic bowls piled high with homemade yoghurt, nuts and lumps of fruit. The eldest, a smooth-skinned black-eyed seven-year-old, wearing a bandanna and a patch over one eye, growled at me and insisted that I walk the plank after breakfast, to which I agreed. As Mitsuko poured my coffee, calmly spooning unpasteurised yoghurt into a bowl for me from a screw-topped jar, Piet entered the room, like a gust of wind, and offered to drive me up to a viewpoint on the Weald.

Steiner-trained, a teacher and storyteller, Piet had already shown an extravagant aesthetic interest in my work, heaping heavy reference books, maps, paperbacks and pamphlets into my arms, finding photographs, imparting quirky snippets of information. He was exhausting to be around, but I accepted his generous offer of a lift up the hill, knowing that he would be a colourful and knowledgeable guide. We walked to the car. I sat in the front seat holding a stuffed parrot and a cardboard cutlass, while Piet clipped the boys into their booster seats. Then we drove for a couple of miles to a gravelled car park, high on Coleman's Hatch Road.

A morning brume hung, like a hazy blue veil, across the vast wooded valley before us: it was a cinematic sight, a fairy-tale panorama of high ridges and steep-sided valleys, scattered farms, fields and hedgerows, heathland, pinelands, boundary beech and mature stands of oak, silver birch and Scots pine. While the boys had a sword fight, Piet handed me his binoculars and began to tell me the story of Ashdown Forest in dazzling detail: how it was once a primeval wildwood covering the post-Ice Age British landmass, how it had been shaped over centuries by man through coppicing, charcoal production and iron extraction, transhumance, hunting, clearing and settlement; that it was a kind of Eden, that it crawled with birds, butterflies and small mammals living in and among the foxgloves and violets, the primrose glades, the bell heather, bracken and vanilla-scented broom.

I held the glasses to my eyes, scanned the dewy landscape as he spoke, breathed essence of pine, fern and damp grass, imagining the dormice, rabbits, stoats, foxes, weasels, squirrels and badgers that were nesting and breeding above and below me in the forest's folds, tracking wet paths of pigmy rush and yellow centaury to drink from gill streams and watering pools bogged with pillwort and three-lobed crowfoot. I imagined the light-footed deer that grazed at the edge of ploughed fields among wormwood and sand catchfly.

The writer G. K. Chesterton once said of the Weald, 'It's where London ends and England can begin,' and for that sweet moment, elevated as I was above all that was green and pleasant, I felt as if I was looking down into the very heart of Albion. I thought about our small island with its varied geology: the Cotswolds, so familiar and so beloved, the Chilterns, the Cornish coastline, the Norfolk Broads, the Somerset Levels, and the spectacular heights of Cumbria, each distinct region with its own rugged or expansive or tranquil or poetically inspiring claim. It's hard to pinpoint any one location and say, unequivocally, *this* is England, but to me, standing there in that morning light, in that landscape, so lush and leafy, so ancient and yet so fresh, I sensed that the sunlit sylvan soul of the Weald was where England truly had begun.

Piet pointed over his right shoulder and called to the boys, who were still play-fighting, asking them to tell me who lived over there: 'Eeyore and Piglet!' they yelled, with wicked delight, in my direction. Piet explained that the author A. A. Milne had once lived on a farm a mile or so to the south of the village of Hartfield: the flora and enchanting wildlife of this timeless paradise had inspired him to create the Hundred Acre Wood for his son, Christopher Robin. 'This,' he announced proudly, with a sweep of the hand, 'is the magical world of *Winnie the Pooh*.' It made me smile to think that the stories read to me by my parents, that I in turn had read to my own children, still appealed so strongly to the next generation.

Gesturing wildly now, Piet took me back to Mesolithic times, described the hunter-gatherers who had moved through the Forest with the seasons, the people in ages past who had farmed, settled and harvested its plentiful resources, the iron industry that had lasted there from before Roman times to the sixteenth century. He lowered his voice, leaned in and told me that, although the smelting furnaces and forges had all disappeared, still, in some places, where the exposed roots of loosely landed beeches rest on smooth boulders, like the veins on the back of an old man's hand, iron-rich water drops between fronds of fern, sealing the stone's surface with a shining russet glaze.

I was loving the theatre, but I was in the mood for walking and felt the need to explore on my own. I thanked Piet for the ride, waved to the boys and told them I would find my own way back to Forest Row. I left them in the car park, walked across the road and gently downhill, heading south on springy grass, the pathway lined on either side by scrub and small trees. I kept going, wishing I had the dog for company, past a bowling green and a cricket pitch on level land, then steeply down to a bridge over a stream and into tall beech woodland, past a coppice of sweet chestnut, pale-stemmed, lucent-leaved, grown in the Forest to make the uneven-edged strips that I'd seen used for fencing here. In all directions, sandways dissolved into the undergrowth with trail-marks of delicate, free-living, fallow deer: a reminder that for centuries this forest had belonged to the king and was maintained as a royal hunting ground.

In 1987, Ashdown Forest was still owned by the De La Warrs of Buckhurst Park, one of those venerable British dynasties that can trace their ancestors back to Domesday and William the Conqueror. At the time of the storm, William Herbrand Sackville, the 10th Earl De La Warr, had decided to sell the forest, after nine hundred years of family stewardship. He offered it first to the local authority, East Sussex County Council, for the bargain price of £1.2 million, threatening to break it up and sell it piecemeal on the open market if they didn't buy it. A public appeal was launched, led by Christopher Robin himself, but before negotiations could begin, the storm blew in from the south-west and within hours, in water-logged earth after days of rain, chestnut and hazel stands were flattened and trees across five hundred acres of Ashdown's forest lay on their side. Veteran beeches, with their shallow, sandy anchor, were the first to fall, their roots like loose ribbons underground.

Lord De La Warr, already fragile, was being treated for anxiety by his doctors. His depression deepened after the storm: the damage, the chaos, the prospect that his forest would simply rewild itself and the cost to put it right overwhelmed him. Like so many others in those early days after the storm, he had no idea how to recover from it. Four months later he threw himself under a Tube at St James's Park.

I turned and made my way back up to the car park. Piet and the boys had disappeared so I tipped over the ridge and dropped down the other side in the direction of Forest Row, heading north on tracks through sunlit beech, birch and pine, and over open heathland, keeping the sun behind me. There was barely a breeze and the crystalline notes of birdsong filled the still morning air.

A bird-watching friend had told me to look out for the Dartford warbler[40] in the Forest: an unobtrusive bird, smaller than a blue tit, with a muted colourway and long tail feathers, the warbler has made something of a comeback to the area, after a series of cold winters almost killed it off in the 1960s. The Forest's vegetation lures it here from Mediterranean climes and it perches on the lowland heather with its red-wine breast, adding its scratching, mechanical call to the flint on flint sound of the stonechat, and to the sweet spring songs of the willow warbler, the reed bunting and the linnet: gorse-lovers, all.

Supremely alert, as they all are, to the earth's natural rhythms and to the volatile forces of the upper atmosphere, many birds would have managed to escape the storm in October 1987. They can sense any slight alteration in the air that fills the tiny sacs positioned strategically about their lightweight bodies and, as barometric pressure plummeted in those hours before the storm, a quivering call to action would have reverberated through every hollow bone and to every barb on every feathered tip, urging them to leave the endangered areas for safer heights.

Birds such as rooks and herons that return to permanent sites in the canopy are known to have suffered long-term changes to their nesting habits, and the strength of the winds displaced many seabirds too. The sight of oceanic species, such as Sabine's and Little gulls, grey phalaropes, skuas, Leach's petrels, kittiwakes, terns and other waders, caused huge excitement in the birding community, as hundreds of unusual birds were blown onto reservoirs and lakes across southern England.

The black-capped Sabine's gulls are pelagic, so are rarely seen inland. After breeding in Greenland and in eastern Canada, their migratory route to over-winter in South Africa takes them across the Atlantic, where they linger in the Bay of Biscay for the autumn months. Until 1987, there had been only four previous sightings of Sabine's in the south-east (the birds were seen at Staines reservoir in September, 1950). But after two adult birds were reported flying west from Hammersmith Bridge at 9 a.m. on the Friday after the storm, the number of Sabine's blown north from Biscay and sighted in fifteen locations over the next five days grew to fifty-two,[41] as they moved upriver to feed on different reservoirs.

The Little gull was the most sighted seabird of all species recorded after the storm, with up to 250 recorded in this one influx alone, and Grey phalaropes, the pelagic waders, were sighted in the rough corners of a variety of west London reservoirs, feeding on insects and debris on the storm-blown surface alongside the Sabine's. Most of the birds counted in this wreck[42] had left the UK in a matter of days, but some Grey phalaropes, Sabine's and Little gulls stayed in and around London for nearly two weeks after the storm.

Twitchers, bird experts and ornithological societies still claim that the clear-up and the aggressive rush to remove fallen trees proved more damaging to birds than the storm itself: but where the canopy opened and where fallen trees were allowed to lie, new habitats were created for birds and other wildlife. Near Sevenoaks the woodlark, a bird that hadn't bred in Kent for many years, began to breed again.

And on a small lake, surrounded with large trees at the end of a long lane in Chailey, East Sussex, something else remarkable happened: here, a family of mute swans, S-necked, orange-billed, regularly and aggressively fought a group of herbivorous Canada geese for control of the watery turf. At lunchtime on 15 October, the warring bird families mysteriously ceased hostilities, left the lake and walked in a long single file, with their young, into the middle of a large arable field nearby, hunkering down together on the ground. The following morning, sixty large trees blocked the lane, cutting off the farm workers' cottages for four days; the disputed lake was a matrix of fallen boughs and sodden stems, the woodland beyond entirely flattened but the geese, the swans and all their young had survived the devastation.

More than half of this forest is natural heath; Ashdown represents 2.5 per cent of the whole of England's rare heathland resource, much of it now under threat from over-development, forestry and agriculture. Since medieval times, the commoners – local people living in and around the forest – had been responsible for maintaining the uncultivated heathland. In exchange for burning the scrub, they were entitled to pasture their swine, collect birch, willow and elder for firewood, and cut bracken and heather for their bedding and roof thatch. After the Second World War, as the numbers of commoners declined so did the health of the Forest, for if humans take even a small step back from this landscape, heathland quickly becomes old and woody, bracken spreads, birch and other trees invade. Now, though, a new era of forest management has taken over, preserving the heath and the wildlife that lives on it. Hardy species of cattle, horse and grazing sheep have been brought in to help maintain the delicate balance between nature and man that has existed here for generations.

I kept walking, kept thinking about poor Lord De La Warr and his forest. In the end, the picture was not so bleak: coppice was damaged and many of the glorious 150-year-old beeches were lost, but those clearing the Forest had employed a prescient lightness of touch. After essential replanting of coppice, many of the fallen trees were left where they lay, like monuments to the ravaged landscape, hosting insects, fungi and lichens, providing cover to ground-nesting birds, returning nutrients to the soil as they decayed.

I arrived back at the cottage to find the boys up a tree in the garden, Mitsuko in the kitchen and Piet in fierce conversation with a bemused walker, his back to the wall on the shady lane. I packed my bags, said a quiet farewell and thank you to Mitsuko, who offered me a gingham-topped jam jar of her homemade yoghurt and a windfall apple for my lunch. I walked to my car, shouted, 'Jolly Roger!' to the boys and drove away.

18

Buxted Park

senses swarmed with buckram bloom
my mind alive with all I knew

I drove south through the Forest. I'd planned to go directly to the coast, to Hastings, but intrigued by a story about a storm-damaged avenue of lime trees, only twenty minutes away, curiosity had nudged me into making an unscheduled stop on the way. On the busy A road, straight, bracken-lipped, tented with towering oak and sycamore, and stippled with early-afternoon sunlight, I rolled through the Wealden towns of Wych Cross, Nutley and Maresfield, followed the signs to Buxted, turned right half a mile before the village and puttered across open parkland towards Buxted Park Hotel.

The flat-topped Palladian mansion, standing in three hundred landscaped and wooded acres on the southern fringes of Ashdown Forest, was, for centuries, a palatial private residence, home to aristocrats, politicians and philanthropists, to celebrities and sheiks. Its most aesthetic owners in the thirties and forties were the architect, designer and colour theorist Basil Ionides and his society wife Nellie, a fantastically wealthy heiress to the Shell oil fortune.

When the Ionides' only son died at the age of nine, Basil and Nellie poured their grief-stricken energies into the house, into lavish parties and unrestrained spending. They crammed the elegant, high-ceilinged rooms with art and artefacts, arranging silver, snuff boxes, ceramics, plaques and priceless porcelains in glass-fronted cabinets, adorning the walls with ton-weight tapestries, French etchings and sketchings of toy poodles, for which Nellie had a declared weakness.

But after fire ravaged the building in 1940, taking with it many of their treasures, the subsequent remodelling of the house was brutal. The original residence was robbed of its roof, its top floor and its generous porticoed proportions, leaving it stunned, stunted and irregular, the architectural equivalent of a headless chicken. Basil, traumatised, died a decade later and is said to wander his beloved abode at night, spooking wedding guests and corridor-creeping conference delegates.

Since 1963, the house has reinvented itself several times: as hydro spa and health club, as home to the president of the United Arab Emirates and now as a hotel, although it wasn't fad or function that had brought me here. As I pulled into the car park, came to a gravelled stop and surveyed the expansive parkland, I did wonder whether I would still be able to find what I was looking for.

Old maps show how this site has been approached from various directions at different times over the years. In the eighteenth century, a colonnade of Scotch firs, three or four trees deep on either side, their thick, straight, scaled trunks rising to more than a hundred feet, stretched from the north-west corner of the park for a third of a mile across the estate. Even earlier than that, at the end of the seventeenth century, 120 lime trees were planted in a long, graceful line to escort horse-drawn carriages to the eastern side of the house.

Planted in 1684, this lime avenue was conceived more than fifty years before the curvaceous landscapes of Capability Brown became fashionable. Until that shift in thinking came, an avenue, a bold arboreal framework with equidistant planting and dappled shade, was greatly admired and much copied. Avenues were thought to focus the mind and control the gaze and were as much a symbol of wealth and status as they were a nod to the great gardens and parks of seventeenth-century France.

On the night of the storm in 1987, 88 of those 120 mature limes in the disused eastern avenue were blown over, falling one on top of another, knocking each other over, like ninepins. Even those left upright suffered broken limbs and battered crowns. But in the frantic, well-intentioned activity of the following days and weeks, as chainsaws blared elsewhere, the great limes at Buxted that had stood for three hundred years lay still and silent on the wet ground. No one came. Overnight the grand avenue was lost. Another storm in 1990 finished off the remaining trees and the site has remained untouched ever since.

I explained what I was looking for to a helpful man on the hotel's reception desk, who pointed me in the right direction. I wandered through the building, from one side to the other, through carpeted lounges with high-backed chairs and glass coffee-tables to a bar where a half-glazed door opened onto a terrace and a flight of stone steps leading down into a garden. I pushed open a tall metal gate and began to walk, as instructed, away from the hotel grounds onto open grassland, towards a lone *Wellingtonia*, droopingly statuesque, and beyond it a rare Hungarian oak.

The pale sedge was spongy underfoot, tufted and uneven. I tripped and dropped clumsily from tussock to furrow until I reached a badger crease, heading downhill towards a trilogy of sunken lakes. I turned left onto a wide greensand flat, hedged by crackling bronze bracken, and kept walking, the shining lakes behind me now, beyond them the River Uck and beyond that, scrubland rising to a heavily wooded scarp.

I was minutes from the hotel, from civilisation, dog-walkers and landscaped parkland, yet time had already drifted back and was carrying me with it. Completely alone, I felt my senses shift and heighten, alert to new sights and signals, to microscopic movement in the undergrowth and to dizzying frequencies of sound. Feeling wild, dissolved and disoriented, my feet cushioned by the timeworn turf, I became aware that I was walking parallel to a dense woodland. Thinking I must have reached the old avenue, I turned and saw, to my wonder, an upturned root bole, its scabrous crust like the surface of an alien planet.

It was at least ten feet high, bedded in brambles, ferns and fallen leaves with soil the colour of biscuits caked to its giant base. Its redundant root system had turned in on itself and twisted into a dark central cavity about four feet up, its craggy outline edge was capped with a layer of velvety green moss. Growing out of the moss, on top of the bole, along the full length and from every side of the recumbent trunk, were broad, smooth stems, each one a lime tree in its own right. Bushy crowns flourished at pollard sites in the fissured bark, and whips, shrubs and seedlings had taken root in the understorey.

Suddenly, before me, I saw the entire avenue of upturned limes, each broad, horizontal trunk sustaining thirty years' worth of vigorous vertical growth, the flattened, decaying undersides subsumed into the earth. I walked on a thick matting of green fern and leaf litter, flanked by the linear lime woodlands on either side: majestic trees, once so ordered, now upturned, the avenue's former formal configuration hovering like a ghost some-where within the unstructured storm-tossed greenery.

In 1987, the time of the great lime avenue at Buxted was already over. The mature trees, decrepit and in slow decline, would have fallen naturally, in time, but the storm had accel-erated and compressed that inevitable disintegration into a single night. I'd read that the lime avenue had been preserved as a Site of Special Scientific Interest since 1989, when three nationally rare species of beetle, another fifty endangered beetles and several scarce flies, including a rare marshland hoverfly, had been discovered among the thousands of insects and inver-tebrates recorded as living on the dead wood and putrid fungi. As well as insects, the site heaves with birds and small mammals, including foxes, badgers and rare albino deer. (I had a private moment of perverse delight when I learned that the preserva-tion order had prevented the whole area being cleared for a golf course.)

In its magnificent decline, this lost avenue suggested much more than straightforward natural regeneration. It felt like natural chaos: wild Nature, in all her anarchic, unsentimental glory. Standing there, a shiver of joy running through me, I was reminded of the places I love the most. I thought of the wild corners and decrepit edges of home: the tangled woodlands, the skyline fields cross-stitched with a thousand miles of crum-bling drystone walls, and the seventeenth-century canal that shadows the River Frome, a long-neglected channel of dere-liction sunk deep into the valley floor.

Looking down the upturned avenue for a final time, I saluted its energy and abandonment. I thought of all the time and ridiculous resources we spend gardening, constantly trying to restrain nature, and yet, if we were all to disappear tomorrow, wildness would quickly reassert itself and surge back, just as it had done here.

19

The Stade

generations berthed and bred
to trammel and sprat,
to voyage in search of mackerel,
fleet for drifting herring,
launch from the beach,
surf ashore,
fish for cod in all seasons.

I tore myself away from the abandoned limes and returned, reluctantly, to the car. I drove north to pick up the main road through the Forest, then south towards the coast, back on track after my wild diversion. An hour later, I reached the battle-ground heights above Hastings and the sky opened out before me. I caught my breath as the road tipped me forwards and rolled me steeply downhill, past Victorian guesthouses, pink, blue and whitewashed buildings with flaking fronts and illumin-ated signs staggered in stuccoed layers on the hill.

The road eventually levelled out and I followed the left fork onto Rock-a-Nore, which is where this town of two halves divides. The other end of Hastings, the western end, is a recently revitalised and bustlingly British seaside resort with amusement arcades, B-and-Bs, grand seafront hotels, a promenade and a spanking new pier, but I was looking for the old town at the eastern end: the home of the largest beach fishing fleet in Europe.

I drove as far along the sea front as I could go, past the Jerwood Gallery, all boxy and black-tiled, with its ground-source heat pumps, contemporary top-lit, white-walled spaces and its collection of modern British art. On into the Old Town, past the authentic working men's cafés, the fish-and-chip shops, the jellied-eel bars and the Dolphin Inn, with its scallop-shell brick-work. Past the quaint entrance to the East Cliff Funicular, fronted by palm trees and Victorian lampposts, past the tall, black-boarded net shops and the Fishermen's Museum in the old chapel to where the tarmac finally peters out and the tottering sea cliffs begin.

The fishermen own this pebbled stretch of seaboard they call the Stade, a Saxon word meaning landing stage, and, unlike their coastal neighbours, Brighton, Worthing and Eastbourne, which lost their fishing livelihoods to tourism, the Hastings Old-Town community fought to keep theirs, here, on a slivered quarter-mile of creeping beach grass, breeze-block sheds and glazed bronze tailings, where their flat-bottomed boats have been stored, launched and landed for centuries.

The shingled roofs of the Jerwood back directly onto the Stade, but this working beach front is an art installation too. Cuttle traps are stacked in tilting piles, four high and fifteen deep, and yellow tractors and tarpaulin-topped troughs of miscellaneous nautical equipment line the gravelled tracks down to the water. Builders' bags in complementary shades of teal, turquoise, beryl blue and seaweed green lie in stuffed heaps among the orange floats and upturned rowboats, fluttering dans and diesel cans, rusting capstans and old white vans. Where the foreshore shelves above the waterline, the vessels perch in uneven formation: the *Wilfie A*, the *Jack Henry*, the *Elsie Rose*, *Senlac Jack* and the *Pioneer*, their hulls bilged and their decks scrubbed, all of them flying the tattered colours of St George.

George became the patron saint of England and protector of the royal family in the fourteenth century, but as a military saint and patriotic figure, he goes back to the eleventh century,

long before the Norman invasion, long before William, Duke
of Normandy, fought Harold, King of England, at the Battle
of Hastings in 1066 – and won. I remember being taken as a
child to Normandy to see the Bayeux Tapestry: a dusky length
of cloth, 70 metres long and more than nine hundred years
old, preserved behind tempered glass in an air-controlled
museum. Its cast of tiny figures, helmeted, chain-mailed and
stitched in ochre, terracotta and gold yarn on tabby-woven
linen, describe the build-up to the most important battle ever
fought on English soil, one that led to the death of King Harold
and, with it, Anglo-Saxon England. Perhaps that was why the
fishermen felt the need to fly the English flag.

After hearing the tragic story of fisherman Jimmy Read, who
had died on the beach on the night of the storm, I wanted to
see the set-up on the Stade for myself, so I'd included Hastings
on my road trip and here I was, on the beach, arriving just in
time to watch a small white boat with a clinkered hull surf up
onto the shingle with its catch.

Black smoke billowed from a pipe on the wheelhouse roof
as the diesel engine powered the little vessel towards the shore,
its keel grinding to a brusque halt on the wet stones. A young
man in yellow-bibbed oilskins jumped from the prow and jogged
up the beach to retrieve a length of broad, rusted chain that
was lying on the ground. He dragged it behind him to the boat,
attaching it to a rope hawser thrown to him by the onboard
skipper, and after he had positioned some planks beneath the
keel and activated the mechanised haul, the boat was pulled
up the steep slope, squeaking over the stones, then brought to
a halt behind the fish shops, steadied, levelled and unloaded.

I stood and watched the whole thing, utterly absorbed. People
strolled past me with dogs and ice creams, their children kicking
balls and throwing casual stones into the sea, apparently oblivious to the live saltwater spectacle being played out in front of

them; evidence, if I needed it, that the daily slide and haul of the boats on this beach is as integral to the life of the town as the shriek of seabirds, the suck and shift of the waves.

I turned and walked along the beach, feet sinking into the deep shingle. Huge herring gulls, with pale orange beaks, balanced, mewling, on beach bollards, on posts and poles, on clanking masts and on the gunwales of fishing boats parked up after the morning sortie. Flocks of fluttering turnstones crept along the pebbled edge of the strand, pecking for molluscs and maggots, and rising above us all, behind the row of low, black-boarded fish stalls, their marble slabs still churning with gasping plaice, was the south face of East Cliff: tall pillars of laminated rock, smattered with green and topped off with the crenellated landing stage of the funicular railway.

I walked towards a pod of fishermen, gathered around one of the boats, deep in discussion, some sitting on plastic crates, others standing, arms folded over bibs and braces. I recognised a couple of them from the large black-and-white images that hang as part of a photographic installation from the buildings along the Stade. Always on view in their ramshackle back yard, every move, every pose a photo opportunity, these men are like celebrities, I thought. In their dungarees and sea boots, they seem unaware of the salted signals of weatherworn style they're sending out, how sensual the slip of their briny harvest.

The fishermen made their views on Europe very clear to me. They were frustrated by unfair catch limits that allowed large, commercial vessels and boats from different EU countries access to their fishing grounds; sick of having to comply with quotas that favoured industrial trawlers while penalising small sustainable fisheries like theirs; fed up with short fishing days, twelve-mile limits and having to throw perfectly good fish back into the sea; angry at being controlled by Brussels, by grey men in suits who were failing to protect their fish stocks. The fishermen told me that the Common Fisheries Policy was devastating British fishing and that, consequently, they would all be voting to leave the European Union in the referendum on 23 June 2016. Now I understood the red and white flags.

Hastings was always a fishing town, in medieval times and before, but its original harbour now lies deep below the shopping precinct of the modern city centre. It's hard to believe that the country's major seafaring ports in the twelfth and thirteenth centuries included the now land-locked town of New Romney, as well as Sandwich, Hastings and Hythe, which, with Dover, completed the line-up of the prestigious Cinque Ports. These medieval harbour towns provided ships and men for the Crown fleet, in return for valuable rights and privileges, commercial benefits and social status.

In 1287, a ferocious storm, even greater than the one that hit the same coastline exactly seven hundred years later, caused a storm surge and extensive catastrophic flooding. Overnight, the shape of the south coast was realigned: the inland town of Rye suddenly found itself by the sea, Broomhill and Winchelsea were washed away; the prominent harbour town of New Romney was left a mile from the coast, its buildings covered with a salted layer of mud, silt and shingle. At Hastings, the sandstone cliff above the town collapsed, taking part of the Norman castle with it, infilling and destroying the protected inlet that served as a harbour. And the coastline is still changing: a transformational geological process called longshore drift, which carries sediments from east to west along the coast at an angle to the shoreline, is responsible for how the Stade looks today, but may not look tomorrow, as climate change brings with it increased water levels, higher seas and more frequent storms.

I asked the men if any of them had been on the beach on the night of the storm in 1987, if they had known Jimmy Read. They all nodded, remembering how they'd gathered to move the boats up the beach in those wild early hours of the morning, how they'd lost and then found their man, taken him up to the hospital themselves on the back of a truck, even though they knew in their hearts it was too late.

One of the fishermen, Peter Coglan, offered to tell me more about his old friend and we walked slowly back along the beach to his single-storey breeze-block shed, set back from the boats and the untidy collection of crates, boulder bags and polystyrene blocks. Stretched along the inside wall of the shed was a length of nylon trammel net that Peter was in the process of mending. Draped in a line from hooks drilled into the wall, the gaps where the net had snapped were visible against the grey brick. It looked like a long job.

The trammel is a three-part net: two taut outer layers, with large mesh, and a slack inner net, with smaller mesh, attached to a floated headline and weighted to drop vertically in the water. The fish swim through the outer mesh and become tangled on the inner. Along with trawling, which uses a cone-shaped net behind a moving boat, it's one of the methods used out of Hastings, the boats dropping between six and eight fleets of trammel nets at one time. Years ago, when the old herring nets were made of cotton, I learned, the mesh broke easily, was quick to rot and needed drying out before it was rolled up and put away. Although the use of nylon lightens the workload considerably for the fishermen, the nets still need regular maintenance.

Peter's shed was a clutter of marine equipment and other random objects: rusting winches and engine parts, plastic buckets and bags, a shrimp net, hanging oilskins, a kettle, some mugs on hooks and a crusty-topped bottle of Gaviscon, half empty. Two high-backed wing chairs had been placed on the concrete floor either side of an old gas barrel that had been converted into a wood-burning stove – the height of recycled chic. One of the chairs was covered with a smart red paisley, the other with an incongruous blue velour, and as a hefty seagull stomped like a man on the felt and tar roof above us, I sat on the blue one, listening to Peter and watching him mend his nets.

The Hastings fishing community is tight-knit, the workforce turnover low, and many of the men working on the Stade today are from the same Old Town families who've fished these waters for generations, the Adamses, the Whites, the Coglans and the Reads among them. Jimmy Read had been to sea, but at the time of the storm he was a 'boy ashore': an integral member of any beach fishing crew. The boy ashore supplies the boats with diesel, collects the fish, takes it to market, and does a bit of maintenance to earn his share of the boat's takings. Before bulldozers were introduced to push the boats to the water's edge, it was up to the fishermen and the boys ashore to launch them, shouldering them over the shingle and tipping them into the sea at high tide. Jim, well, he was an asset to any crew, being the strongest man on the Stade by far.

Peter's family have history in this place too. The youngest of three sons, he, his father and both his older brothers all went to sea and now, with two sons and nine grandchildren of his own, he's confident the tradition will continue – he's even bought a new boat for them to make sure it does. Technology may have changed the way some things are done, not least the nylon nets, sonar equipment and the replacement of cloth sails with diesel engines, but some things will never change: knowing where the fish gather and why, knowing which season brings cod and which sole, and what time of the day or night to catch them. These things are passed from one generation to the next, a fishing father's legacy to his fisherman son.

Peter drew me a map of the coastline between Beachy Head and Rye Harbour and filled in the colourful names of some of the sandbanks and submerged rock formations that have provided him with rich fishy pickings over the years: Back of the Sand, Hole in the Sand, the Hards, Hooks Hards, Cliff End Hards. He said that some of the older fishermen know instinctively where to stall their boats and drop their nets, that they still navigate by markers on land, such as trees or church spires, which tell them where they are at sea and where the shipwrecks lie.

It's this intuitive knowledge and the centuries of tradition that keep the fishing community strong. What's more, in an era of over-fishing and unbalanced quotas, the Hastings men are proud of their sustainable methods, using wide mesh nets that allow young fish to escape, ensuring a continuation of fish stocks for future generations. Why would they want to do otherwise, when their children's tomorrow depends on the way they fish today?

Turns out that in the sea around Hastings, especially where the local waters of Rye Bay border the busy Channel, the preserved hulks of hundreds of ships lie in the soft sand of the sea bed, enticing different fish at different times of the year to feed on the millions of mussels and limpets that grow on them. Around the Goodwin Sands alone there are about a thousand ships, thought to be the largest concentration of wrecks in Europe, most of them dating to the nineteenth and twentieth centuries, but many from much earlier eras too. Even further back, before the last Ice Age, when sea levels on the south coast were about ninety metres lower than they are today, dinosaurs roamed in a prehistoric forest on the Hastings foreshore, the traces of which can still be seen at low tide.

The modest fleet of twenty-nine boats based at Hastings today hardly compares to the glory days of the mid-1800s, the industry's period of greatest prosperity: fleets of deep-sea luggers trawled from January to April, drifted for mackerel till late July, then for herring till Christmas, often spending weeks away at a time, combing the waters from Land's End to the Scottish border. Now they catch sole and trap cuttlefish in the summer, no more than twelve miles from shore, landing mainly cod, skate and plaice the rest of the year. The long-distance fishing trips are gone but, although some weeks there's barely a living to be made, the fishermen of Hastings refuse to be shunted or shut down.

Jimmy Read might have been taken on land, Peter told me, but his memory is held just as close by the fishing community as if he'd been lost at sea. The clinker-hull fishing boat he owned at the time of his death was restored and donated to the Fishermen's Museum by his wife and, every year since the storm, the whole community remembers him with a bike race through the Old Town, asking people to cycle up Crown Lane, as he used to, without ever taking their backsides off the saddle.

The following morning, I woke early: another B-and-B, another unfamiliar bed, a snip of daylight in the gap between the curtains. I thought of the Hastings fishermen, already six or seven miles offshore, nets dropped, engines on tick-over, the only other sounds the call of sea birds, circling above them, the waves slapping against the hull and the hush of the wind. This, their daily intuitive act of faith and harmony with the sea, launching their boats from the beach in all seasons, so naturally in tune with the moon and the earth's turning.

20

The Apple Orchards of Kent

*The restless apple journeys west
with bolts of cloth and saffron threads,
as fodder and in merchants' vests,
pilgrims' pockets, donkey dung.*

I checked out and drove due north of Hastings on the A21, then followed the luscious road back across the Weald towards Hawkhurst, diverting briefly to see the medieval castle at Bodiam. Another National Trust property whose ancient woodlands had been damaged in the storm, its fat, fantasy towers were reflected, like a submerged Camelot in the still green waters of the moat, as if nothing had ever happened.

By now, I was running behind schedule: I would have to resist the romance of Sissinghurst Castle, the russet-brick, towered and turreted home of the writer and gardener Vita Sackville-West, which also lay on my route east. I knew that its formal gardens would be white with lupins, hostas, alliums and agapanthus, that its waving butter-cupped meadows would seduce me with their amaranthine flat-mown paths if I let them – but, bravely, I held my course and drove past.

I'd needed a little help to find apple farmers in the south-east who remembered the storm and who would be willing to talk to me about the lost harvest of 1987. I'd come across a wonderfully informative website called the English Apple Man, an online guide to all aspects of apple production, enabling consumers to 'understand the challenges English growers face in supplying our sophisticated market place', and I'd contacted

John Guest, the charming and well-connected English Apple Man himself. He had put me in touch with two Kentish fruit growers, both of whom had agreed to talk to me.

To the Tassell farm in the red-stone village of Ulcombe first: an ancient settlement in a hollow on the side of a hill, in the heart of this fruit-growing county. Charles invited me to climb into his Land Rover – a mud-splattered workhorse, seats covered with heavy-duty cloth, footwells mugged with clods of earth – for a bumpy tour of the ancestral lands that had suffered so badly on the night of the storm.

Wheels spinning and sticking in the rutted tracks, we drove steeply uphill to the flat sandstone field above the farmhouse, now fallow, where hundreds of young Gala apple trees had been lifted and tossed over a windbreak, then back down to the lower acreage, where the ferocious winds had bulldozed every last tree to 45 degrees, leaving an entire orchard of Bramleys leaning at a grotesque angle to the earth.

When Charles and his father had first seen their mutilated orchard, the morning after the storm, they noticed that, although most of the trees had broken roots on the windblown side, almost all had retained enough root in the ground to allow them to recover naturally. 'We decided to leave the mature Bramley orchard on its side,' he told me. 'The trees were certainly deformed, but we knew the rootstock was strong. The leaning stems seemed to be defying gravity, hanging stiffly and without support in mid-air, but with some cute pruning and clever shaping, taking the weight from the boughs that hung nearest to the ground, almost all of the trees survived and continued to fruit healthily for another eight years.'

The field had been through numerous agricultural cycles since then – arable, fruit and grass. Now, however, it was let to one of the biggest commercial fruit farmers in the area who, as I was about to see, had recently planted a 'fruit wall': a high-density system of apple production, in which fruit grows quickly and profusely in tall, narrow hedgerows and can be harvested two or three times in a season.

We sat in the Land Rover, Charles and I, looking out over misted Kent countryside that rolled hazily downhill and into the distance before us. On one side of the field, in an orientation from north to south, and on the other from east to west, ten-foot-high poles stretched in straight lines for as far as I could see, each pole dug into a mound of raised earth and strung to its neighbour with strands of thick wire, fastened at two-foot intervals from the ground up.

Between the poles were pale bamboo canes dressed in knee-high stockings of silver mesh, each supporting a single slender apple whip, tied in with fluttering green tape. Twenty-five thousand newly planted apple trees over ten acres, Charles told me, at least 80 per cent of them Gala, methodically drip-fed by a complex irrigation system, the scrolls of black piping cradled in hidden trenches underground.

The planting, picking and cold storage methods of the commercial fruit industry have changed out of all recognition since 1987, and a new breed of super-grower is now emerging. 'These giant fruit producers rent land from smaller-scale farms, like ours,' said Charles. 'They plant fields of raspberries. They have cherry trees under nets, strawberries on table tops in poly tunnels, and now these apple walls too. They invest heavily in advanced planting and harvesting techniques to achieve higher yields per hectare and to meet the demands of the supermarket.' He added, 'They're also more environmentally conscious than ever. They've done away with the old chemical baths and sprays and have embraced organic methods of pest control to meet strict new environmental guidelines.'

Even I could see that the intensification of production was transforming the commercial fruit-growing landscape. The traditional orchard had, long ago, given way to the uniform planting of dwarf trees, with low, open branches, but now many of those are being supplanted by these ten-foot-high walls of fruit; long rows separated by a network of grass super-highways, wide enough to take mechanical picking machines.

We drove back to the farm and parked in the yard for a tour of the old warehouses, built by Charles's father in the fifties, when cold fruit storage was still rudimentary, the corrugated outer walls painted a faded agricultural green. Back then, the apples were picked, wrapped in plastic, covered with straw and left here, in the cold shed, with open bags of lime absorbing the carbon dioxide in the air, thus preventing the fruit from ripening.

We walked through sliding doors into the dimly lit, crudely insulated chambers. Outdated they may be, their basic functionality long overtaken by hi-tech scrubs and carbon-dioxide-filtration methods in purpose-built storage units, but not yet redundant. There was a grey frigidity to the air and a distinctly horticultural aroma emanating from a stack of wooden crates, full of flaking flower bulbs imported from Holland. The bulbs were being stored here in arrested development, as apples once were, until they were ready to be dispatched to garden centres all over the country.

With their fertile acres farmed for them, and with many of their outbuildings now home to light industry and small businesses, it's the rent and the diversification that enables farming families to hold on to their land. 'Realistically,' Charles told me, 'the margins in arable are now so small that you need at least two thousand acres to be viable, and as far as fruit production is concerned, the costs of picking, packing and storage and the continual investment needed to keep up to date with new technology and planting methods are huge – but it's precisely what the giant fruit producers are able to do with their vast economies of scale.'

I drove onwards to meet Sandys Dawes in the village of Hernhill, near Canterbury, reflecting on the many changes to the fruit-growing landscape over the past thirty years. Gone are the tied farm-workers' cottages and the orchards that provided year-round work for local families. Gone is Kent's hop production and the colourful itinerant picking culture that went with it, and gone the traditional orchard, the unwieldy, widely spaced and misshapen trees, the uneven sward, the hedgerows humming with wildlife.

Gentlemanly and softly spoken, a teacher by training, Sandys inherited the fruit farm at Mount Ephraim from his father in 1982, moving his family into the big house and opening the twelve acres of formal gardens to the public. We sat together in the family kitchen, drinking coffee and looking at faded photographs from October 1987. At that chaotic moment, Sandys had taken the calm and far-sighted decision to document the aftermath of the Great Storm, with a collection of images that now offers a unique historical record of an extraordinary event.

We climbed into an old pick-up and Sandys drove me around the estate, the management of which has now passed to his own son. The rows of short, squat apple and pear trees, the hundreds of cherry trees under netting, with their distinctive oval leaves, their slit bark, may give the orchards here a more traditional aspect than the progressive fruit walls I'd just seen in Ulcombe, but, as Sandys explained, Mount Ephraim has always been a progressive operation. One of the first farms to adopt the new trend for strawberry table tops in 1996, several years later it had also taken an unconventional leap and expanded into cherries, which is now their predominant fruit crop.

We talked about attitudes to the storm and about the financial implications of losing a harvest, as many farmers did in 1987; how some had seen the destruction as an opportunity to grub up and replant their orchards, update their methods and start again, while others were forced, or chose, to get out of farming altogether. 'Storms aside,' Sandys said, 'protecting fruit from pests and disease is probably the greatest challenge fruit farmers face today.'

With increased globalisation, the casual shipping of live material in vast commercial quantities means that alien dangers continue to arrive daily in consignments of fruit and other food from distant countries. When living things leave their own environment, they invariably bring diseases to which indigenous organisms in the destination country have little or no resistance.

Growers of soft fruits are particularly anxious about a vinegar fly from South East Asia that eats the fruit from the inside out. The nasty little spotted-wing drosophila, *Drosophila suzukii*, arrived in the UK from North America, via South America and Japan, and although it can be controlled by permitted pesticides, the longer the sprays are used, the more resistant the pest becomes.

But garden plants and woodland trees are just as much at risk: I'm old enough to remember the disappearance of elms in the late 1960s: the gaps in the landscape after Dutch Elm Disease's slow dispatch of an estimated 30 million mature broadleaved beauties over a twenty-year period, after infected elm logs were brought into the UK.

The Forestry Commission's current list of 'top tree diseases'[43] makes sobering reading. Ash trees suffering from *Chalara*, ash dieback, have been dying in their hundreds of thousands across Europe since the disease was first detected in 1992. There are almost as many ashes in the UK as there are people and yet, if the *Hymenoscyphus fraxineus* fungus takes hold here as it has done across Europe, it has the potential to kill them all.

The emerald ash borer, a beetle native to East Asia, could be the next major threat: introduced to North America in wooden packing material in the 1990s, it has already spread across the US and Canada and is now moving west from Asia at a rate of forty-one kilometres a year. In the UK, across the south-west, South Wales, Cumbria and in Scotland, larch trees too have shown great susceptibility to another fungus-like pathogen, *Phytophthora ramorum*, also known as Japanese larch disease, although it also affects northern red, holm and Turkey oaks, as well as beech and sweet chestnut. With statistics like these, I'm not sure just how good a protector of the world's plants and trees we are proving ourselves to be.

We drove back to the house, past a derelict, roofless building at a crossroads, buddleia stems growing carelessly out of the tumbledown walls, the knitted tubular flower heads, like purple socks. 'That's the old oast house you saw in the photographs, the one that lost its roof in the Great Storm,' Sandys explained. 'It had already lost its original function by 1987 and was only used for storage and as a place for the seasonal fruit pickers to sleep, but it's been left to disintegrate for thirty years now and, as you can see, it's just a ruin.'

How huge and voracious our demand for fruit, I thought, as I left Kent in the late afternoon for the long drive back to Gloucestershire, my road trip at an end, the setting sun slumped, fat and pink, in the sky ahead. How complicated food production has become, how crafted and controlled the landscape, how unpredictable and compromising the increased exposure to pest and disease. But equally, how reassuring to see the old oast house with its nettle skirts, its creeping mantle of ivy: to know that Nature will always reclaim what man chooses to leave behind him in the name of progress.

PART 5

LEGACY AND LOSS

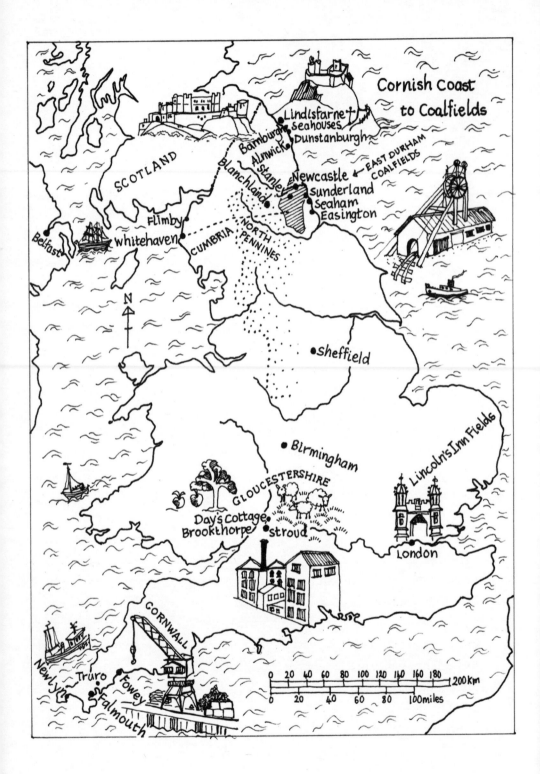

Cornish Coast to Coalfields

21

Day's Cottage

GLOUCESTERSHIRE
Summer 2016

discarded cores insinuate,
intent on germination, wait,
rot and root and vegetate
on hoofmark, track, receptive verge

I left the house and stood outside, coated, booted, the dog dancing at my feet. I walked up the narrow, high-hedged lane, alert for any oncoming cars rounding the corner at speed, reached the field and wedged through the kissing gate, brushed by hip-high fronds of cow parsley. I slipped the dog's collar and let him make his matinal checks and balances, then walked up towards the playing field and the perched village of Randwick, with its panoramic view of all five of Stroud's valleys.

It was early summer and the trees were in sail, a pair of gigantic field limes, and an English oak, waving unevenly in the gentle breeze from their lowest branches to their twisted tops. I walked underneath a beech, could almost feel its pulse, as it drew hundreds of gallons of water from the earth into the tips of its glossy leaves. The hedgerow was fat with field maple and spiny hawthorn in wedding white; dogwood and elder jostled for space on the pitted ground, where blackbirds, hungry after their dawn exertions, picked and shuffled among the twigs and dry leaves.

Stroud's an old wool town that lies in the shape of a crumpled star at the point where those five valleys meet. The iron-pillared halls and flagstone floors of its textile mills still echo with industry, and the springs and small rivers that once powered hundreds of gigs, looms and carding machines drop sharply from high wold to vale, under low clouds soft as lambswool. They call it the Golden Valley, for the vast sums of money that were once made here, but the phrase could just as well be used to describe the luminous stone of the vernacular buildings, the heavenly light that filters through its beech forests or the gilded tones of the trees in autumn.

On the playing field, a young man smoothed the cricket pitch with a heavy-duty grass roller, headphones plugged into his ears, a red jersey tied around his waist. Affiliations of brown-eyed rabbits darted from tump to bramble, teasing Scout, my half-hearted collie, who gave up chasing them long ago and now simply watches as they vex him with their feint and speed. Silver-capped jackdaws dropped from their roosts and bounced onto the path in front of me; chaffinches chattered under the hedge.

I walked back towards the house on the usual paths, ending up alongside an old orchard. Since witnessing the industrial activity in the commercial orchards in Kent, I'd found myself looking at the veteran apple trees in this field with new eyes, seduced by the gnarled and irregular stems, the gaping holes in the trunk you can push your hand into, by the high-hanging clumps of mistletoe, the resident buzzard, the restorative atmosphere of silent seniority.

The orchard with its Tolkien-esque relics is a remnant, I'd learned, a torn-edge memory of how it used to look around here before the farmer sold the land for a housing estate in the late sixties. When we first moved here, our new neighbours had us round for a drink and showed us their collection of old photographs: faded black-and-white images of our eighteenth-century hay barn, its great doors ajar; the old cider house, its tiled Cotswold roof already speckled with lichens; and their own handsome farmhouse, as it used to be, ringed by cider orchards. They told us that there were once hundreds of apple trees, all the way down to the brook at Puck's Hole, then up to the top of the hill and for as far as the eye could see.

I found old Ordnance Survey maps of Gloucestershire from 1842 that showed orchards, just like these, all along the banks of the River Severn, as far north as Evesham and across the county. The landscape changed after the Second World War, when housing developers became hungry for land and supermarkets began to demand homogeneity of shape, size, colour and taste in the apples they chose to sell. The radical changes in land use and farming practices led to the disappearance of 75 per cent of the county's traditional orchards, as they were grubbed out, sold off or modernised, in favour of the same factory-like production I'd seen in Kent.

The stillness of the morning air was broken by a series of spasmodic thumps, and I noticed that the orchard was crawling with activity. A couple of battered green Land Rovers were parked in the lane, and at the edge of the field, two men were hammering wooden stakes into the ground, laying a hedge of bare-root saplings – blackthorn, wild cherry, field maple and hazel – within a deer-proof fence. In the orchard itself, another man was carefully planting new trees alongside the resident elders, building rustic square guards around the fragile stems. I recognised him immediately: it was Dave Kaspar, a traditional fruit farmer from Gloucester who, with his partner Helen Brent-Smith, is a familiar figure at the farmers' market in Stroud. I'd always admired the apples on their stall, the vintage crates with their loose seasonal cargo, coarse- or smooth-, russet-, carmine- or blush-pink-skinned, each variety with its own distinct aroma and crunch. I loved picking the ones I wanted, smelling them, holding them and hearing them drop into the brown-paper bag.

Dave told me that the old fruit trees were Bramleys and Newton Wonders, and that the landowner had asked him to revitalise the orchard with twenty young apple trees in traditional Gloucestershire varieties, which included Arlingham Schoolboys, Lodgemore Non Pareil, Beauty of Bath and the famously delicious Ashmead's Kernel[44].

We stood and talked for a while in the sunshine. I told him about my recent visit to Kent, spoke of commercial fruit walls and vinegar flies, of storm-blasted orchards and the lost apple harvest of 1987. Dave asked me if I'd like to visit them at Day's Cottage, to see how traditional orchards are managed, by way of comparison.

A few weeks later, delighted to be invited, I drove from Randwick over the ridge and down the hill to the village of Brookthorpe, on the flat, fertile river plain, south of Gloucester. I parked the car beside the house and took a moment to lean against the wooden paling at the edge of the home orchard, grazed since the Middle Ages and sheltered by beech woodland on the Cotswold scarp above. The venerable centrepiece was a high, hollow-stemmed pear tree, more than three hundred years old, its early white blossom over, its sloping branches in heavy green leaf.

Fruit has been grown in orchards like this since Domesday, with trees in rows, twelve yards apart, on wildflower-rich, uncut grass that mimics forest pasture. Fruit trees develop veteran features much earlier than other types of tree, and in traditional orchards, like this one, the gashed trunks, split bark and rot holes are ideal habitats for nesting birds, roosting bats and burrowing beetles. But as landscapes have changed, as old orchards have disappeared, and as the use of pesticides has increased, there's been a marked and worrying loss of that wildlife habitat.[45]

Inside the house, at one end of the kitchen, what looked like a woollen scarf was in fact an aged cat, asleep on a computer keyboard. A neurotic collie barked, then eyed me warily from her bed by the door as Dave and Helen welcomed me in. After pushing aside piles of papers and clearing a space for the coffee pot and three mugs on the long kitchen table, we sat and talked under a low-hanging light, warmed by the unseasonal thud of heat from a vintage Rayburn, a row of mismatched socks draped over the handrail.

Day's Cottage is a successful small business with a loyal clientele, fifteen productive organic acres of apple and pear trees, and five of perry orchards. Dave and Helen are founder members of the Gloucestershire Orchard Trust, a charity that offers advice on the conservation of traditional orchards. They run workshops on all aspects of orchard management, passing on their wealth of hard-earned knowledge and making sure that traditional skills survive.

The couple left London in the late eighties, their move to Gloucestershire as much an expression of social protest as it was environmental conscience. She was a psychologist, working with the homeless and the abused, he a linguist, teaching French and Spanish at a comprehensive school. They were frustrated idealists, they told me, swimming against the tide in a consumer-led society and increasingly disillusioned with Thatcher's Britain. They railed against the hour-counting, the withdrawal of goodwill and the lack of trust, their hard-earned profession-alism questioned and micro-managed at every turn.

In his youth, Dave was a budding Gerald Durrell: the son of a Czechoslovakian spy, he was a rugged romantic who dreamed of escape, of living in a cave or returning to the land.

Helen, on the other hand, had watched her own parents work themselves into the ground on their own West Country small-holding and had no illusions about how hard a rural existence could be. Finally, however, in 1989, they made a stand: they pulled out of London and moved into this tumbledown cottage in the middle of a field.

She made things out of papier mâché and he did a bit of supply teaching. They grew organic vegetables, kept goats, chickens and pigs and, in the autumn, collected windblown apples from the two old orchards behind the house, either giving the fruit away or leaving it in wooden boxes at the farm gate, asking passers-by for honest pennies. The first two years were hard: the little cottage was dark and draughty; they had no money and lived on baked potatoes and fresh air.

In 1991, unexpectedly inspired by a weekend course in permaculture and encouraged by a massive crop of Bramleys and Newton Wonders in the home orchard, they decided to make better use of the land around them: the apple and pear trees might have looked untidy but they were, at least, a product-ive resource. They made plans to revitalise the orchards that were already there and create some new ones on their twenty acres of British soil.

Twenty-five years later, their commitment to what they call their 'green, idealistic vision' has paid off. Though they are experts now, back then, they admit, they were just a couple of academics, 'winging it'. With no one to tell them how things should be done, they taught themselves how to prune, graft and juice, and hoped that intuition, hard work and a respect for the land would be enough.

I was struck by the timing of their story. From what I'd seen and heard in Kent, it seemed that the storm of 1987 had been something of a turning point for fruit farming. The late eighties saw an inevitable rise in intensification that signalled the end of traditional practices and small family fruit-growing concerns. At the other end of the ecological scale, however, the storm also coincided with a shift in mood towards caring for the environment, both at home and abroad, of which Dave and Helen's brave leap in 1989 was a part.

The Slow Food Movement began in Italy in 1986 when a group of impassioned Romans, protesting against a new franchise outlet of the American burger giant McDonald's, succeeded in stopping the development, drawing international attention to the erosion of local economies and to non-sustainable food production.

In 1987, as our storm-damaged woodlands were being bull-dozed, cleared, tidied and replanted (and as David Russell was asking, 'What happens if we do nothing?'), the visionary arts and environmental charity Common Ground[46] was adding its voice to calls for a more natural recovery to the disaster, printing and distributing fifty-six thousand postcards illustrated by the environmental artist and sculptor David Nash. Nash's message that a fallen tree is not necessarily a dead tree, encouraged people to view the apparent chaos as an entirely natural event, to which there would be a natural response.

Two years later, in Gloucestershire, Charles Martell, a farmer, cheese-, cider- and perry-maker, embarked on drawing up a new 'Pomona': an inventory of the 190 different varieties of Gloucestershire's apples and their characteristics, with the aim of reintroducing old varieties to orchards around the county. In October 1990, in response to the increased globalisation of food, the intensification of food production and the demise of local produce, Common Ground, again, introduced Apple Day, an autumn event to celebrate local food and its benefits to the community and the landscape. They asked that people look again at the riches in their home environment and value the vernacular, particularly the contribution traditional and community orchards make to local distinctiveness.

The Italians' distinction between fast and slow food, the idea that what we choose to eat has an impact on the earth's resources and the health of the consumer, and the resurgence of interest in traditional orchards, all chimed with Dave and Helen's personal protest, vision and instinct. From 1997, as the number of farmers' markets increased, promoting local, sustainable produce, so too did Day's Cottage sales of organic juice and apples.

All fruit farmers, whether commercial or traditional, face problems with pests and disease and Helen described at least two years of despair, as bugs ate through their newly planted orchards, shredding the leaves and crucifying the crop. Even when faced with the total loss of their orchards, their policy of non-intervention and trust in the land meant sitting the crisis out, to be rewarded, in time, with a new flush of growth on the affected trees and a healthy crop the following year.

For modern commercial fruit growers, operating in a completely different environment and on a much greater scale, trusting nature to restore her own balance in this way is not an economic option. Continuity of supply is essential if global markets are to meet the insatiable year-round consumer demand. It's a demand that Helen and Dave, working in the way they do, know they could never fulfil. They acknowledge that intensive farming methods are necessary for the wider market and here to stay, but the environmental and social promise they made to themselves almost thirty years ago won't change: their passion, patience and belief in the land today is the same as it was back then.

'But it's no rural idyll,' said Helen, with feeling. 'It's physically exhausting, all-consuming and intense. There was a very good reason why man moved away from the peasant lifestyle that tied him so inevitably to the earth and to the seasons. Apple trees live for about eighty years and need constant maintenance and replanting. Raising traditional varieties means getting to know the individual characteristics of each tree, their likely yield and each one's susceptibility to pest and disease. There's grafting to do, fruit to pick, to box, juice, market and sell. It's hard, seasonal, outdoor work and the demands of the business are never at an end.'

Even so, I was instinctively drawn to the rustic enterprise at Day's Cottage. I admired Dave and Helen's environmentally friendly working practices, their dedication to the cultural and aesthetic value of orchards, the way they live and work with the seasons. My conversation with David Russell still resonated, as did Aldo Leopold's call for mankind to reshape its relationship with the natural world.

Dave and I left the house and walked a few hundred yards along the lane into what they call their 'Museum Orchard', an impressive, seven-acre field planted in 2007, with 200 trees in eighty traditional Gloucestershire varieties: slender trees, carefully pruned into curving, upward boles with names like Elmore Pippin, Jackets and Petticoats, Flower of the West, Gilliflower of Gloucester, Hens' Turds, Taynton Codlin and Parlour Door.

The wide-spaced trees were canopied with a delicate white blossom; the avenues sloped gently uphill towards young beech and oak woodland and a disorderly row of painted wooden beehives. 'We've got bee-keepers queuing up to keep their bees on our land,' Dave said. 'They pay us back in jars of organic honey. What's not to like?'

We stand and survey the idyllic scene. 'These apple trees are young and still a couple of years from fruiting,' he said, 'but with their average life expectancy of eighty years, we like to think they'll still be here long after we're all compost.'

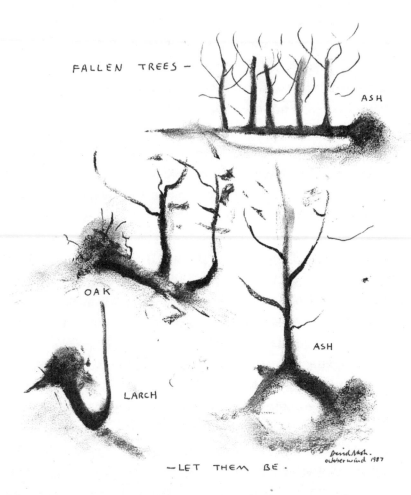

FALLEN TREES —

ASH

OAK

LARCH

ASH

— LET THEM BE .

David Nash.
Octoberwind 1987

22

The Science of Towage

The cable sings, tightens, snaps.

Captain Paul Thomas, retired Royal Navy sea captain and Fowey harbourmaster, stood at ease in the bay window of his book-lined office, the steeply wooded estuary edge behind him like a stage set, yachts sliding smoothly past, languid in the morning breeze.

'The crucial element of a ship under tow,' he told me, 'is the catenary, which is the U-shaped curve a chain will make if it's supported at both its ends. To get a tow under way, the ship will pay out a length of chain, usually the anchor chain, or two hundred metres of cable, depending on what they've got. That chain is dropped vertically from the ship's bow and the tug's towrope is attached to it. The rope disappears off the back of the tug, the weight of the hanging chain forms the catenary in the water between the tug and the ship, pulling the ship forward and acting as a shock-absorber.'

I listened intently, scribbling in my notebook, freakishly delighted at the acquisition of a whole new vocabulary. This was my chance to learn about the science of towage from an expert: to discover how ocean-going tugs, such as the *Markusturm*, are rigged to pull ships like the *Flushing Range* and the *Gaelic Ferry* half way around the world; to understand how those ships were lost to mountainous seas in the Bay of Biscay on that fateful October morning in 1987.

Captain Thomas continued, 'Hundreds of rigs, platforms, dumb barges and ships, just like the *Flushing Range* and the *Gaelic Ferry*, are towed all around the world, all the time. If they have no engines and no crew aboard, we call them dead ships.'

Over the past couple of months, I'd tried, and failed, to persuade any of the large deep sea tug companies, whose high-horsepower tugs specialise in long-haul marine transportation of windfarm components, offshore oil rigs and marine dredgers, to let me join them on a six-month sea journey from Zeebrugge to Taiwan. I'd explained the nature of my research, I'd even offered cash, but none of them seemed to want to take me along for the ride. I'd turned, instead, to somewhere a little closer to home.

I've been coming to Cornwall all my life. Brought to Falmouth as a child, I spent family holidays here with my own kids, too. These days, I come for windswept walks on the basalt and granite coastal paths around the Lizard, or for wine-soaked weekends in the small harbour town of Fowey. I'd often watched the small, manoeuvrable Fowey harbour tugs pull heavy cargo ships up and down the narrow, deep-water estuary and I'd written to the Harbour Office to ask if anyone would be willing to answer my questions about towage.

And although the small Cornish tugs bear no resemblance to the ocean-going, twin-screw *Markusturm*, and though Fowey, with its daisy chains of dinghies and sailboats bobbing and clinking on the water, is a million miles from the congested maritime expressways of the Channel and the volatile depths of Biscay, I was about to learn that the science and principles of towing a ship remain pretty much the same, wherever you are.

And this is what I'd learned so far: that towing at sea is not like towing a car. You can see the tug and the vessel, but not the rope between them. The towrope should never go taut; the bight – the join between the ship's chain and the towrope – should never break the surface of the water, but if it does, the tug's speed must be reduced or the towing line lengthened.

'Here, in the estuary,' said Captain Thomas, 'we keep a fairly tight control on the ships we bring in. For deep sea towing, however, and to avoid snatching and wear, the catenary is best kept six to nine metres below sea level, and dropped to about 12 metres in rough weather.'

Throughout the tow, he explained, the chafe must be kept to a minimum by wrapping the hawsers (towropes) and lining the fairleads[47] with canvas, lubricating them with liberal amounts of soft soap or grease. At sea, the steering gear on the ship under tow is set to midships, although there will always be a certain amount of veering, depending on the swell and on the strength of the wind. In stormy conditions, however, such as persistent one-hundred-foot waves in Biscay, serious tension can be created in the towrope.

'When the ship under tow starts to drift and yaw excessively,' said Captain Thomas, 'snatching can cause the rope and chain to part and the tow to be lost: which is precisely how the *Flushing Range* and the *Gaelic Ferry* broke away from the *Markusturm* during the storm.' He added, 'The crew were able to recapture the ships several days later, so emergency tows[48] must have been rigged before leaving port.'

To me, the idea of being in a boat, at the mercy of those one-hundred-foot waves, was a terrifying one. Would the crew of the *Markusturm* have been scared? I wanted to know. 'A seafaring person wouldn't be scared,' said Captain Thomas, coolly. 'Let's just say that he would consider conditions such as those a "challenge".'

He went to the bookshelf, pulled out his copy of *The Admiralty Manual of Seamanship 1983* and turned to the chapter on towing in open sea. 'There are a number of ways to rig two ships, one behind the other,' he explained. 'I suspect the *Ferry* and the *Range* were under tow with a device called a bridle: chains on both sides of both ships, connected to a master chain from a hydraulic steel winch on the tug's deck. As the ships drift and yaw, the tug's chain pulls them back to centre.'

And what about navigational technology? I asked him. How sophisticated was satellite navigation in 1987 and what alternative systems might have been available to long-distance sailors? 'Although there would have been limited satellite information', Captain Thomas replied, 'sailors relied more on either Loran C[49], a receiver that picked up low-frequency signals from land-based radio beacons, or on a phase-timing radio system known as Decca.'

Neither navigational system gave full ocean coverage after Lisbon, at which point the captain of the *Markusturm*, like any other sailor heading down into the south Atlantic, would have reverted to his nautical charts: sea maps showing the oceans of the world as charted with plumb lines, bottom dredges and open-water trawls by eighteenth-century hydrographers, nineteenth-century oceanographers and the Royal Navy.

Captain Thomas fetched one of his own sea charts and rolled it out on the long table, weighting each of the corners with a leather-bound book. Delicately coloured and exquisitely drawn on heavy stock, the map described the maritime area around Fowey: it showed the coastline, detailed tide times and navigational hazards, such as sandbanks, rocks and sudden drops. The *Markusturm* captain, like any true mariner, would have had his charts stowed in canvas sleeves on shelves in the wheelhouse, but if these, and all else failed, he would have returned to his trusted sextant[50], relied on dead reckoning and celestial navigation, steering his ship according to the position of the stars in the dark night sky.

Captain Thomas then asked if I'd like to see for myself how

a tugboat operates: he was expecting a cruise liner into the estuary the following day and, if I could muster by 5.15 a.m., I could join tug captain John Burgess and crew for an educational ride.

He didn't need to ask me twice. I booked myself into a B-and-B – was barely able to sleep for dreams of toppers, tankers and tall ships – and was woken at dawn by gulls barking on the nearby beach at Readymoney Cove. I tiptoed outside to where my hostess, Jenny, had strung a hammock between two rustic stakes on a terrace, and lay on my back looking up at the plum-black sky, listening to the perpetual ebb and wash of waves on Cornish shingle below.

At 5 a.m., guided by a solitary day star, I tiptoed out of the house, along the Esplanade, down into the salted folds of the sleeping town and along Fore Street, the pad of my shoes on worn tarmac and the faded flutter of bunting the only sounds. Past the unlit gift shops and restaurants, the chemists, clothes shops and cafés, past Albert Quay, its granite harbour walls tickled by the darkly rising tide, past the handsome house with the shell porch and up along the dank corridor of North Street, with its holiday homes and Wesleyan chapel, to where the road opens out onto Caffa Mill.

I crossed the deserted car park and stood at the top of the Bodinnick slipway where I'd been told to muster: I was alone, but the shifting silt of the river bed sang with the souls of smugglers, pirates and privateers, and in the steep, sombre woodland that shadowed the slopes behind me, I sensed a host of 'phantom listeners'; felt just like Walter de la Mare's lonely traveller, 'knocking on the moonlit door'.[51]

John Burgess appeared at the top of a flight of steps in his short-sleeved white shirt, decorated with the navy and gold epaulettes of the Fowey Harbour Patrol. He handed me a lifejacket and I followed him through a gate and down to the water's edge, where half a dozen bleary-eyed men, the tugboats' crews, were huddled on a pontoon, hands in pockets, waiting to board a small motor launch that was tied up alongside.

One by one, we stepped down into the boat, the engine roared, and we curved away from the mooring in a perfect arc, up the estuary to where the tugs, the *Cannis* and the *Morgawr*, were waiting. I pressed my feet down into the flats of my shoes and clung to the gunwale, swaying and steadying with the little boat's every lift and dip, trying to look as if I'd been born on water. My fellow sailors were silent. I could hear them thinking, *Who the hell is this woman?* but they asked no questions, so I simply returned their curious sideways glances with the most reassuring smile I could summon in an open, fast-moving boat at that hour of the day.

We motored past a wharf piled with scaffolding, chutes and conveyor-belts, where a vast cargo ship, the *Lady Christina*, Dutch-registered, her welded steel hull painted patriotically orange, was being loaded by men in boiler-suits and bandannas. Fowey is a port that handles at least 750,000 tons of china clay every year, brought in by rail or road from the drying plants at Par and loaded onto industrial barges, like this one, until they sit so low in the water that they must wait for high tide before they can sail back down the estuary and out into the Atlantic.

We jumped off the launch onto the pontoon, climbed aboard the tugs and waited for the huge 1,200-horsepower engines to start up. Diesel smoke puffed from the funnels in black belches as the early-morning sun lifted over the horizon and rose, like a peach, into a backlit blue sky. I sat upon a faded leather bench, high on the bridge of the *Cannis*, with John at the wheel, steering her up the estuary, the *Morgawr* not far behind. We dodged yachts, motor launches and fishing boats tied in clusters to orange buoys, chugged past Albert Quay, waved to a lobster fisherman in a flaking wooden boat, and saw a white-haired man swimming in the clear shallow waters off Readymoney Beach.

As we reached the harbour mouth, where the ruins of a castle on the Polruan rocks oppose the Gothic mansion at Point Neptune across the estuary, I thought admiringly of Roger Deakin, the writer, environmentalist and maverick, wild-water swimmer, who'd set out to swim his way around the British Isles, recording his experiences in his book *Waterlog*. Roger chose to cross the River Fowey from this cold deep-water point, but soon fell foul of a coast guard in a motorised launch, who reprimanded him for not seeking permission for his swim from the Harbour Office, and ordered him to return to shore. (Undeterred, Deakin managed to squeeze past them on his second attempt, the following day).

We pulled up alongside the 28,000-ton, ten-decked cruise liner *Silver Whisper*, waiting to be brought safely to its mooring in the estuary for the day. It was early, but a few of the liner's

380 American passengers were already awake and leaning over the metal balustrades waiting to watch the well-rehearsed procedure from the comfort of their private balconies.

The huge ship towered over us. It seemed inconceivable that two small boats could take this monster anywhere at all. Captain Thomas had sailed ahead in the pilot boat, had boarded the *Silver Whisper* and was already in control at her bridge. John explained that the pilot's local knowledge, his understanding of the estuary's currents, its depth and width, was vital: that his main job was to protect the other boats on the estuary from big ships, like this one.

'The captain of any large ship arriving or leaving Fowey hands control to the pilot, who then directs the operation from the bridge and keeps in touch with the tugs' captains by radio,' he told me. 'Depending on the size of the ship, there might be three or four tugs involved in a move. As the tugs can't see each other, they rely on the pilot to coordinate the manoeuvre.'

As Sandy and Ben, two of *Cannis*'s crew, assembled on the lower deck, John talked me through the hitch-up process. A thin messenger line was thrown down from the liner and knotted to the end of a thick rope that snaked across the deck from an industrial reel, like a bobbin, then hauled back up to the high deck of the liner and secured to the ship's chain.

I saw the winch turn and the solid hemp line move through the huge steel staple down below. After a series of brief coded conversations between John and Captain Thomas, the *Cannis*'s engines powered back up, smoke thumping from her yellow funnels. We began to move up the estuary, catenary submerged, the cruise liner behind us, gently weaving, like a giant puppy on a leash.

Hands on the wheel, gear set to midships, lights flickering on the control panel, John's concentration was intense. The engines growled but progress was unbelievably slow. 'Is this as fast as we go?' I asked him, as the tug chugged stolidly forth. 'Depending on location and conditions,' he replied, 'the average towing speed is five knots.'

I tapped the figures into the calculator on my phone: five knots = 5.7539m.p.h. The long, laborious extent of the *Markustrum's* six-month sea journey from Zeebrugge to Kaohsiung was suddenly made real. 13,164 nautical miles, travelling at the equivalent of a brisk walk – sometimes slower. Any faster and the bight would surface, cause excessive movement and put extra strain on the towrope. All I could see behind us was the liner's vast white hull: her prodigious size above the waterline a reminder of the tug's responsibility, the inevitable depth of her keel an indication of this narrow estuary's depth.

We arrived at the liner's mooring point: two rusting rocking barrel buoys on the far side of the estuary. I watched the ship's massive anchor clank, scrape and drop, saw the chain shorten and the *Silver Whisper* pull against it, finally settling, coming to rest. Once the ship was secured, the towropes were dropped and Ben and Sandy pulled them over the side in order to winch them back in.

We left the Americans to their continental breakfast and John steered the *Cannis* back to the pontoon. The sun was at its bright morning height, the ferry across the estuary to Polruan was already up and running and a team of hardy women in tracksuits were out for a practice row in their racing gig[52], puffing and blowing loudly.

Scott, the *Cannis*'s engineer, handed me a pair of ear defenders and invited me to descend a metal ladder into the oily green depths of the engine room, where he would show me the tug's two, vertical rotating Voith Schneider engines, like a pair of food mixers in underwater cages. He explained that the downward spinning action of the two engines made the tug highly manoeuvrable and easy to position: 'She can change from full ahead to full astern in five seconds and can stay in one position if required, in the same way that helicopters can hover in the air.'

I told Scott the story of the *Markusturm*, described how the *Flushing Range* had made her bid for freedom during the ferocious storm in the Bay of Biscay, all those years ago. Scott could confirm, from horrifying personal experience, that conditions in Biscay can often be atrocious. His first job as a young ship's engineer had been on one of the Cornish fleet of tall ships that are moored in Charlestown's picturesque wet dock; his first long sea voyage was from Charlestown, across Biscay to southern Spain.

Less than a day into the crossing, he told me a vicious storm had blown in from the west, seemingly out of nowhere. The tall ship, taking one to two feet of water every hour into the bilges, lashed by waves that topped her 140-foot mast, and ill-equipped to cope with the onslaught, surfed the waves at double her normal speed ahead of the gale, for three full days, before the wind and rain abated. Scott was so violently seasick during the three-day storm that his only option was to chain himself to a metal strut on the shrinking wooden planks of the open deck, where he could vomit freely, which he did, until he was barely conscious, thinking the nightmare would never end. 'I've never been sea sick since,' he smiled.

Standing in the hot and stuffy glassed-off side section, I found the smell of marine oil almost overwhelming. 'We use diesel,' said Scott, 'but in 1987 they would have used heavy oil, which is cheaper and more economical, but much less refined.' Using a ton of heavy oil per day, he told me, an ocean-going tug such as the *Markusturm*, with the capacity to carry hundreds of tons of fuel, could get from Zeebrugge to Cape Town on just one tank. Re-fuelling could be effected at sea, using one of a network of fuel barges, or by using the bunkering service at one of the larger ports en route.

Later that afternoon, when the American passengers had returned to the *Silver Whisper* from their jaunts to the Lost Gardens of Heligan, the Eden Project, or from playing nine holes at the nearest golf course, and with onlookers ten deep on the quayside, I climbed aboard the *Morgawr* to accompany Captain Thomas, John, Scott and the rest of the crew as they performed the whole procedure, in reverse. They towed the liner, by the stern this time, to the mouth of the estuary, before turning her full about and sailing alongside her, as she made her way towards the Atlantic shipping lane. I felt the thrust of the spinning engines in the bowels of the tug, as finally we circled, changed direction and chugged back up the estuary and home.

That evening, back at the B-and-B, I switched on my computer and logged on to a global marine-traffic website that shows the seas and oceans of the world and all the ships that are upon them in real time. I lay in Jenny's hammock as the cloudless sky changed from Byzantine blue to aubergine, mesmerised by the luminescence of the live map, the bright clusters of red, orange, turquoise and lime-green arrows, thousands of them across the face of the earth on my little screen, each arrow a container ship, a liner, tug or tanker. For each arrow clicked, a drop-down menu appeared showing a photograph of the ship in question, giving its status and destination, distance travelled and the number of sea miles still to go. I found the *Lady Christina*, with her cargo of Cornish clay, 'underway using engine', already in the Dover Strait on her way to Estonia, and there was the *Silver Whisper*, on her way back to Southampton, after her luxury round-Britain cruise.

And I looked out at the wide, dark horizon and the bound-less black sea rising to meet it. I thought of the Dutch captain of the *Markusturm* in his wheelhouse, being guided down into the south Atlantic by nothing more than celestial light, the ignominious journey to Taiwan resumed. I imagined the tug moving by inches over unfathomable depths, oil lamps burning on the decks of the two recaptured vessels, tipping, yawing and creaking in her wake. The *Flushing Range* and the *Gaelic Ferry*, discredited, disobedient, but brought to heel at last.

23

Falmouth

For the slow sound of you,
the salt song of blood in your veins,
your ocean breath,
a prophetic tune played shallow
on crusted half pipes.

The following day, I gathered my things, said goodbye to Jenny, took a bus to Par station and caught the slow train to Falmouth to visit my aunt Joy. I wanted to explore my father's creative legacy and the mysterious origins of his artistic talent, and his older sister was the only person who could tell me what had raised him, shaped him and shot him off, like an arrow.

The final inland stretch of the Great Western line clips Truro to the north of the city, in glorious sight of the three-spired Gothic Revival cathedral; it clatters cross-country, and skirts the northern edge of the Fal estuary, before dropping to Penryn and steeply down again to Falmouth town and the docks. The Friday morning carriage was eclectically full: half a dozen chattering school girls in blazers, a young mother with a baby in a buggy, a couple of art students, spooning, he with bleached hair in a bun, she pucker-lipped, devoted, her ears, nose and eyebrow delicately pierced, and next to them, an elderly man in mud-splattered green wellingtons carrying a pitchfork, the prongs of which were sensibly wrapped in folded cardboard and tied with green string.

Descending from the carriage at Penmere felt like stepping back in time: vintage brown railway signage with raised cream lettering, a single platform overlooking a blowsy field of red campion and ox-eye daisies, and an old-fashioned silence that settled over the track, once the train had tickered into the distance. I followed the Way Out sign to a car park where a taxi was waiting to take me to Beacon Road, a street of small, white-washed terraced houses and palm trees at the top of the town, with views east over Carrick Roads, the Fal estuary and Falmouth docks. I got out of the car, then took a moment to breathe and look around. I hadn't been there for years, but it still felt familiar.

Joy opened the door, smiled and looked at me, searchingly. She told me she'd forgotten what I looked like and asked, only half joking, was I always this tall? Straight away, I heard him in the way she spoke – the softly curling Cornish accent, the distinct-ive, almost combative turn of phrase. I saw her face, contoured as his might have become, her eyes like his, fierce, intelligent, vulnerable, their edges creased with humour and with pain. I remembered looking at her from across the church at my father's funeral in 1998: tall and slim, an unceremoniously-dressed woman in a plain skirt and jumper, her auburn hair flecked with grey, and I remember thinking then, ah, yes, there I am.

We'd met again a couple of years after that, but in the long, slow readjustment to life without him, and without him there to keep the communication channels flowing, our good intentions to stay in touch had gradually dwindled, reduced to a Christmas card once a year and, some years, not even that. But I was here now and I wasn't going to let my emotions overwhelm me, even though they were threatening to. I followed her into the house, where we sat, politely at first, speaking and listening, in turn.

At the mouth of the Penryn River, on a curve of land protected from off-sea southerlies by the Pendennis promontory, Falmouth is the third deepest natural harbour in the world[53], a location that has defined its role as a focus of waterborne trade for

centuries. The famous Falmouth Packets carried mail all over
the world until 1851; pilchards, tin and corn went out by sea;
timber, iron and coal for the mining industry floated back in.
Carrick Roads is a deep, sheltered stretch of water, bordered
on three sides by patchwork fields, footpaths, mature woodland
and small fishing villages nestling on its inland creeks, coves
and tributaries, the estuary of the Fal River, which opens onto
the English Channel at its southern end.

Falmouth played an important role during both world wars:
minesweepers and Q-ships, troop vessels and convoys were
based in the harbour during the First World War, and casualties
from the Front were transported here in their thousands to
special reception centres and hospitals. Between the wars, there
was huge expansion: new engineering shops, improved berthing
and cargo handling facilities, and the enlargement of two of
the dry docks, making them the biggest in Britain. With an
increase in both naval and merchant shipping, there was plenty
of work for all kinds of skilled maritime tradesmen.

The town grew up and away from the harbour onto the
steep hillsides above the town. The wealthy had already moved
out, bought vast estates, built manor houses set in ornamental
parkland, with sweeping drives and fine gardens. Town housing
continued to boom: hotels and guesthouses were built, as were
fine stuccoed villas and semi-detached houses with bay windows,
and industrial terraces for the workers, higher up.

'Your great-grandfather, William John Thomas, was a
Cornishman,' Joy began, 'who left Falmouth in the late eighteen
hundreds to look for work and raise his family in County Down,
Northern Ireland.'

But political division began to spill into all walks of life in
the 1920s, when the fault lines which had opened up over
Home Rule began to re-emerge, after a fragile truce during

the First World War. William's youngest son, Alfred Henry, my grandfather, decided to leave Ireland and return to Falmouth with his brother Eddie, to find work in the docks. 'He was working there as a boilermaker when he met your grandmother, Margaretta Gladys Kelynack[54], a fisherman's daughter from the village of Newlyn.'

Joy pulled a Quality Street tin towards her and levered off the lid to reveal a stack of old photographs. 'He may have been a boilermaker,' she said, 'but he always dressed like a lord.' She was right: high-quality three-piece suits hung handsomely from his tall, slender frame, accessorised by Homburgs, silken ties and a watch chain strung from his waistcoat pockets. Gladys had been equally fashion-conscious, it seemed: conspicuously talented with the needle from a young age, she made all her own outfits – white cotton shirts, wool suits with brass buttons and deep pockets, and floppy felt tam o' shanters. I looked closely at a faded image of the two of them, sitting together atop a Cornish rock: manual workers maybe, but as handsome as old-time movie stars.

They were married at the Centenary Primitive Methodist Church in Newlyn on 10 August 1929 and moved straight into their new home on Beacon Road, where, in the back bedroom in 1930, Joy was born, followed twenty-three months later, in June 1932, by Terence Alfred, my father.

Both parents worked. Gladys, a seamstress and dressmaker, had a skill that far exceeded the straightforward patching, altering and mending of clothes that were necessary during the war. She worked with crêpe and silk, made sateen dresses and peach-skin skirts, moleskin coats and flannel trousers in a workshop in the town, her piping, patterns and embroideries confident and creative. 'In the fifties,' Joy said, 'we used to get home from school to find her in the front parlour making wedding dresses, swallowed by billows of white tulle and lace, a Woodbine always hanging off her lower lip.'

Alfred had followed his father into the shipyards. One of six children, he'd had no option but to earn, but the glowing academic reports and Sunday School certificates that had travelled with him from Ireland, packed like precious china in newspaper and kept in cardboard boxes in the attic, were a dusty reminder of what might have been, had he been born to another century and into different shoes. Alf wanted to know everything, and everything he heard or read was processed and stored. He loved history and language, had a curious and analytical mind, an aptitude for mathematics and a blistering ambition that no son of his would ever work in the bowels of a ship.

A child in wartime, Joy remembered the 'friendly invasion' when American troops camped in their hundreds on the Beacon in preparation for D-Day. She remembered the gun emplacements, pillboxes, barbed wire and mines on Falmouth's sandy beaches – Gyllyngvase, Castle Beach, Swanpool and Maenporth. She recalled taking the ferry from the Prince of Wales pier across to the Old Quay at Flushing, pitching tents among trees on the edge of open fields at Trefusis Point. Thereafter, Joy's had been a lifetime chronicled in Cornwall's hidden coves, on its rugged Arthurian promontories, and in the steep streets of this good harbour town.

Her wistful almanac of memories began to slide and lock with the same stories my father had told me long ago. I saw how the landscape had defined them both, created a shared atlas of affinities and affiliations, given their lives shape, orientation and meaning; how that sensitivity, that deeply rooted sense of place had somehow breathed into my father an appreciation for all his subsequent geographies, all his landscapes.

Daily life at Beacon Road revolved around the fireplace: Alf would sit with his pipe on one side of the hearth, Gladys on the other with her sewing, and the two children would sit on hard chairs at the table with pencil and paper, drawing, always drawing, fire burning, radio on. Joy said, 'From the moment he picked up a pencil, your father knew how to draw. His was a precocious natural talent, a God-given gift that emerged in early childhood and took us all by surprise. He saw how light gave shape to things from the start, knew instinctively how to hold a pencil, understood form, colour, perspective, how to make a picture. Something happened to him when he was drawing. It took him away from us, somehow.'

His artistic talent far exceeded that of his masters and there was nothing anyone could teach him at school, so it was his passion for all sport, Joy told me, especially rugby, that carried him through his days at Falmouth Grammar and beyond.[55] I thought how hard it must have been for her to have a younger brother so carelessly talented, (although she said they were always close) and even harder when, already married, with a child of her own and living with her in-laws, she'd watched his inevitable departure when he was eighteen years old.

But his choices would always take him away: with a natural aptitude for languages, he was one of a tiny minority selected for Russian-language training in Portsmouth, when he turned up for his Royal Navy National Service in 1950.[56] A year spent in the German city of Kiel, north of Hamburg, posted on a frigate stationed in the Baltic, intercepting coded Cold War messages from Soviet submarines would open his eyes to the wider world.

When offered either a place at the Slade School of Art in London or the chance to play high-level rugby at St Luke's Teacher Training College in Exeter (run by a rugby-mad principal who selected his students on sporting ability), he chose the latter. In 1957, after meeting my mother at a school in Greenford, west London, where they were both teachers, he moved from London to Lincoln, from there to North Wales and finally to Gloucestershire, keeping time and distance between himself and his old home town.

I found my father's lack of interest in formal art instruction striking: more than just a maverick expression of character, it was, I suspect, indicative of an emancipated desire to follow his own creative path. For having rejected the Slade, he then also ditched art teaching as soon as he could, seduced by a sales job with Guinness that was padded with paternalistic perks such as cars, houses and generous pension schemes, and which promised to pay him double his teacher's salary. Liberated from the institutions of art, he was now free to paint without restriction, which he continued to do for as long as he lived. Prolific and compulsive and with innate casual brilliance, he experimented endlessly with scale, shape, form and line, on board, canvas and paper. He responded to his changing landscapes, finding equal inspiration in the wild Welsh mountains as in the hidden green corners of the Cotswolds: as happy throwing colour into abstract squares on huge canvases or painting life-sized murals, as he was sketching in pencil, washing heavy cartridge with colour or scratching crowd-pleasing caricatures on scraps of paper with dried out felt-tipped pens.

And now I could take up Terry's story. I recalled how, as children, he built us Indian canoes, a tree-house complete with ladder, lookout and timber walkway, a climbing frame, a small fort with painted flags. Requisitioning our sunny playroom in the house in North Wales, he installed his easel, his three-legged stool, a moth-eaten velvet sofa and an assortment of ladder-backs and threadbare armchairs. He stacked square stretched canvases against the wall, splattered the linoleum floor with paint and laced the air with heart-stopping fumes of white spirit and with his drifting cigarette smoke.

I described how his pictures had been integral to my own family's narrative, charting the too-short time we all had together: how I cherished the clever one-line portraits of my three children, sketched in haste with felt-tipped pens on mauve sugar paper; the smiling, tail-less, cartoon donkey that he drew for a birthday party, the delicate watercolour portraits he painted for their bedrooms – the Owl and the Pussy Cat, Jack and his Beanstalk.

And I spoke of how, since he died, I've spent whole summers in France tracing his steps, driving the same straight roads south that he drove. How I stay in the same house under the cherry trees, drink iced glasses of rosé from an earthenware jug, feel the same sun on my back, listen for golden orioles, watch for hoopoes and red squirrels and sit where he sat to paint, gazing at the same sun-bleached towns and villages of the Languedoc.

The taxi arrived to take me back to the station and I hugged my aunt, said goodbye, promised to write, to visit again soon. I settled into a window seat on the train, the swiftly changing landscape a reflection of my fast-moving thoughts.

When I started this journey, I should have known that my father would be waiting for me at the other end, with the answers to my questions. For now, I understood why Cornwall has always had me in her nets: why she speaks to me in a runic language that both charms and terrifies; how I'm bound, skin, scale, gut and gills, to deep water and dry dock, to full moon and low tide, to my seafaring ancestors, to the women of Newlyn and to the huers and hawkers of Mounts Bay. I also understood that if, for reasons of class, expectation, obligation, and against the inescapable backdrop of world history, the ambition, intelligence and creative abilities of my grandparents had remained largely unexplored or frustrated in their own lifetimes, they had, undoubtedly, found a natural expression and far greater opportunity in the next generation: in their exceptional son, my beloved father.

The train rattled on through Cornwall, skirted the southern edge of Dartmoor, hugged the Devon coastline, sped through Somerset, then north from Bristol to Cheltenham Spa, but my windblown journey wasn't over yet: I still had one more place to go.

24

Seaham, County Durham

CHRISTMAS
2016

royalties of coal
seven miles out under open sea

The small north-eastern town of Seaham has been boldly regenerated in recent years, almost all physical reminders of its 150-year mining heritage now concealed or demolished, remembered only with blue plaques and potted information on simple notice-boards. The modern streetlamps, the strategically placed wooden benches with views across the bay, the contemporary sculptures and newly paved Promenade are a world away from the blackened pithead buildings, towering chimneys and bleak architecture that once dominated the seafront.

I leaned against the painted metal railings and looked out to sea, to where filaments of cloud straddled the flat blue horizon. In the distance, shellfishing boats hastened home to the Scottish greystone harbours of Buckie and Blyth, while bulk carriers and cargo ships inched north towards Grangemouth and Peterhead. Below me, bank-holiday anglers in fishing green, bait boxes crawling, rested their tapering rods on the seawall. Joyful dogs dipped to the dew claws in wet sand, dodged and gambolled on the sheltered beach, chasing tennis balls and bouncing into the waves. The cold salt air stung my eyes and slapped my cheeks till they smouldered. All the same, I liked the way the winter sun had staked its fierce claim, lengthening and lightening the days so soon after the solstice.

I'd spent Christmas holed up in a hotel in the Northumbrian village of Blanchland, storm clouds scudding north across Pennine skies, the wind a constant low roar at the shuddering sash windows. On Christmas Eve, in a grave-cold abbey, I sang carols with the moorfolk: red-nosed men in tweed, children in berets and leather-cuffed riding jackets, babies in pink snowsuits with built-in gloves, dummied against fret and fiddling. A flamboyant organist made us sing 'While Shepherds Watched' to the tune of 'On Ilkla Moor Baht 'at', and a lady vicar with a deep voice whisked us smartly through the service, lest we turn to ice on her festive watch.

In the hotel, chickens roasted on spits in the medieval fireplace. I drank northern ale and Durham gin, ate sausages dripping pale fat like liquor onto piles of salted sauerkraut. On Boxing Day, it snowed, and I walked through the village, partridges cackling in the bracken. I climbed over high stiles to wander through barren stands of ash, alder and birch, and back to the hotel on spongy, gorse-edged river paths, like bogs, the fast-running water of the Derwent dark as slate.

The next day, I left Blanchland and drove east to Seaham, through conifer stands, ploughed fields and open heath, following an open-topped Land Rover, with its cargo of surly shooters in earthen breeks, tweed flat caps and waxed jackets, their resting guns pheasant-ready, their tasselled knee-highs a confusion of dusky pink, violet and cherry marl.

The scenery changed as I drove through Shotley Bridge and on to the old mining village of Stanley, where hilltop rows of red-brick colliery housing, skirted by bungalows and characterless estates, ribbon the landscape all the way to Sunderland. I arrived at Seaham's harbour café in time for mid-morning coffee and an iced slice of fruit cake, conscious of my solitary southern reserve, among large groups of friends and families sharing festive tales, the air a-murmur with gentle Geordie voices.

For months now, I'd been living with the story of the homeless man, killed by a falling tree as he slept in Lincoln's Inn Fields on the night of the storm. After some detective work, I'd traced him back to Seaham and I'd been eager to make this journey, stand on this seafront, and see for myself the gritty civic buildings, the districts of Dawdon, Deneside and Dalton-le-Dale.

But I had another reason for wanting to visit this part of the world: while trawling through parish records and census reports in my search for the identity of the homeless man, I'd uncovered a previously unexplored family history of my own that placed *me* firmly up here with my maternal ancestors in the Durham coalfields.

I'd discovered that my great-grandfather, Gibson Carruthers, born in Flimby on the Cumbrian west coast in 1876, was a miner, the son of a miner; that his wife, Hannah, was a miner's daughter and that all her brothers were miners too. Gibson and Hannah had made the eastern overland journey from Flimby to the Durham coalfields to look for work in 1901, stopping and settling at Stanley, only twenty miles short of Seaham, where there was colliery housing and plenty of work in the pits.

I'd revived childhood memories of my maternal grandparents, Gibson's only son James Carruthers and his wife Lillian. They were an immaculate pair, Jim and Lil: she in straight skirts, silk scarves and quarter-length mink coats, her silver hair whisked into an efficient chignon; he in knitted waistcoats with leather buttons, belted trousers creased with perpendicular precision over shining brogues. I remembered childhood visits to their home in Ealing in the late sixties: their spotless back kitchen, the splutter and steam of the pressure-cooker, every hidden corner on every shelf dusted, every surface wiped with a dry-wrung dishcloth.

I'd been mesmerised by my grandfather's teeth, his real ones swapped at the age of twenty-one for a double rack of lustrous porcelain dentures, and by my grandmother's pendulous ear lobes and heavy pearl drops, by her triangular patent handbags and the hollow slap of their metal clasps. I treasured the Premium Bonds she bought me from the post office, the half-empty glass-stoppered bottles of melancholic scent, the real fox fur stole with its beaded eyes and dangling paws that smelt of moth balls, the grey gabardine pencil skirt she gave me when I was a student. But what I loved best was to hear them talk, the way they called me 'pet', their short vowels, their glottalised *t*s, the way they said my name, Tam-*sin*.

I realise now that I only knew them for who they were then, not for what they had been: a miner's son and a haberdasher's daughter from County Durham, whose worldwide cruise and bridge-party lifestyle only began after they'd left the north-east in desperation and poverty in 1930, marching south with thousands of others in search of work, settling in Ealing and never going back.

The plight of the rough sleeper in London's Lincoln's Inn Fields was perhaps the most poignant of all the storm stories I'd heard. He'd died where he slept that night, in the open, covered only with wet cardboard, owning nothing but the clothes he stood up in. Homeless and apparently nameless, too, for while the other seventeen fatalities were all swiftly identified, their tragic stories told and told again, each given national status as a storm victim, the 'vagrant' crushed by a plane tree continued to remain anonymous in all reports and, when the news cycle inevitably moved on, was completely forgotten.

I'd searched everywhere, finally coming across his name, by chance, in a book written immediately after the storm in 1988.[57] I'd contacted the Coroner's Office in the London Borough of Camden straight away, where the administrator confirmed that the deceased's full name was Terence Leo Marrin, that he was sixty-four years old and that he'd died from a crush injury to the head. She told me that the coroner had returned a verdict of accidental death, Camden Social Services had arranged for a parish funeral and, although there was more information on the file, she was sorry but, as I was not a family member, I was not entitled to see it.

But it was a start: the mystery of Terence's life, the wretched circumstances of his death, his unclaimed body and his un-attended parish burial had already moved and intrigued me in equal measure. Even with such scant details I felt sure that I'd be able to discover even more about him; that, after all this time, it was now up to me, somehow, to give him back his identity. I delved into history books and public records and, slowly, the tentative outline of a forgotten life began to emerge.

Six miles south of Sunderland and thirteen miles east of Durham, Seaham was once a barely inhabited 'sea hamlet' perched on coarse maritime grassland above steep limestone cliffs, breakered by the North Sea and buffeted by onshore winds. With the neighbouring agricultural settlements of Silksworth, Ryhope, Murton, Hetton, Haswell and Shotton, and with one of the oldest surviving churches in the country, Seaham remained fundamentally unchanged until the early part of the nineteenth century.

But ever since the Romans had settled and excavated for coal up there, mining had shaped the landscape. As demand for the black stuff grew, it was Newcastle, with its shallow seams along the banks of the Tyne, its established transportation routes by river, sea and later by rail, that became the glinting eye of British coal production, providing the ever-increasing amounts of fuel needed to drive the engines of industrial and social change.

For many years, surface and bell pits had been mined inland, but in the 1820s, when advances in steam-engine technology allowed for the draining and exploitation of deep seams, new mines, some of which stretched out under the sea bed for up to seven miles, were sunk all along Durham's eastern coastline.

First at Murton, then Seaton and then, in 1849, at neighbouring Seaham, the new mine shafts, a mile from the sea and within sight of Sunderland, were the second and third deepest in the country. There were constant problems with flooding and quicksand, and only six weeks after the first coals were drawn at Seaton, hacked out by bare-chested men still working by candlelight, six people died in an explosion. The youngest victim, Charlie Halliday, a pit boy, was barely nine years old.

One of the worst mining accidents ever recorded happened at the Seaham colliery, known as the Nack, on 8 September 1880, when a huge explosion rocked the mine and the surrounding area, blocking the deep shafts with debris, setting fire to the engine house and stables, suffocating at least 180 pit ponies, instantly killing many men and boys, trapping others in remote pockets and inaccessible seams for hours, until the air ran out. That day 164 died, leaving 107 widows and 259 children without a breadwinner. An appeal was launched and raised more than £13,000; apparently Queen Victoria chipped in £100.

But the hunger for the vast mineral wealth that lay beneath the sea and the blown brown landscape in glistening, vestal veins was sweeping aside old farming communities, seducing hordes of miners, like the Gold Rush forty-niners, to Seaham. Small, strong, wiry workers, talking a language of their own,[58] whose large families demanded housing, hospitals, transport, shops, churches, cemeteries, pubs, public baths, prisons and schools.

They arrived in their thousands: experienced miners from other mining communities in the neighbouring counties of Cumberland and Northumberland, from the depressed and dying lead and tin mines in Cornwall and from the impoverished agricultural areas of Norfolk and Suffolk. And when successive potato crops failed in Ireland in the 1840s, millions emigrated. Many sailed across the Irish Sea from Ulster to the busy port of Whitehaven in Cumberland, making the onward journey east to the Durham coalfields on foot.

Seaham's harbour expanded and its rail transport links were improved; the apparently unlimited coal reserves under the North Sea called for another pit to be sunk at neighbouring Dawdon in 1899, and in 1923, a third colliery, Vane Tempest, was built on the Seaham seafront. The industrialisation of the land around the primitive settlements and across the region was unstoppable and unsympathetic. In 1913, with coal production peaking at 41.5 million tons, a staggering 165,246 people were employed at 304 Durham pits. And while the landed gentry, pit owners, merchants and transport providers got fat on the profits, the miners continued to live in overcrowded, squalid slums, working long, dirty, dangerous hours, deep underground for pitiful wages.

Born into this scarred landscape and into extreme poverty in 1923, Terence Leo Marrin was the fourth of six children, the son of a miner, William Marrin, whose own father, Richard, also a coal miner and a Catholic of Irish descent, had arrived in the town in 1884, (having made the same overland journey from Whitehaven as my own great grandfather, Gibson). On arriving in Seaham, Richard moved into 17 South Railway Street, where his wife Isabella produced thirteen children, five of whom died before the age of five. Terence's father, William, was born in 1886 and as soon as he left school (almost certainly before he was ten), he followed his father into the pit.

There were thirty-four poor-quality colliery houses in South Railway Street, one of a grid of red-brick terraces near the seafront, hastily erected to accommodate that huge influx of miners and their families, who'd arrived in the town in the mid-nineteenth century. The houses were all the same: small, unhealthily overcrowded and lacking in ventilation, with one room upstairs, divided into separate sleeping spaces for boys and girls, and another downstairs, where the family cooked, ate and bathed, and where the parents slept.

Water was collected in buckets from Seaham's only water source – a pump at the bottom of neighbouring North Railway Street – the stinking dry-closet privy was in a dark shed outside, and the backyard opened onto a rat-infested alley. Three public houses on the same street serviced the working men after their shifts: The Golden Lion, The Duke of Wellington and the malodorous Northumberland Arms next to the railway sidings, where raw sewage was kept in open carts and taken periodically by rail on a single track to 'Tip Ends' at the furthest end of the sea wall, for the contents to be dumped into the grey waters of the North Sea.

When war broke out in 1914, William, aged twenty-eight,

had already been working underground full time for almost eighteen years. At the end of the war, in 1918, he married Ethel Proctor, moving a few doors down from his parents to 10 South Railway Street, but by the time their fourth child, Terence, was born, the grim terraced houses were in a desperate state of neglect and disrepair (they would be demolished within the decade under the Slum Clearance Act of 1930).

There was a bleak inevitability to the lives of William and Ethel's six children, Richard, William, Kathleen, Terence, Isabelle and Stella: inured to seams, slag heaps, black-faced men, back alleys and the persistent foul smell of industry, theirs was a woefully short childhood. Having watched their father drop to pioneering depths and daily danger in a metal cage, the boys were destined to do the same, and after a few cursory years' education at the local school, the girls found work in the town's bottle and brick factories[59], their contribution to the household income essential.

The history of Seaham's mining community and of my own family was well documented, but Terence Marrin's paper trail appeared to have come to an end. I was no closer to knowing how or why he'd ended up in London forty years later, sleeping rough in Lincoln's Inn Fields on the night of the storm. As a fact-finding exercise, it was rudimentary, and as an attempt to restore a dead man's lost identity, it was frustratingly incomplete, but I wasn't ready to give up just yet. As a last resort, and with genuinely little expectation of any response, I wrote a clutch of letters, explaining my professional interest in Terence, and sent them to anyone with the surname Marrin, living in and around the Seaham area.

Within three weeks, a letter arrived: unfamiliar handwriting, postmarked Sunderland. I took a deep breath and tore open the envelope. Two photocopied newspaper articles fell to the floor. I picked them up, put them to one side and sat down to read the accompanying letter.

The author introduced herself as Jenny, Terence's daughter-in-law, married to his eldest son, Sid. She apologised for her delay in replying but she'd needed to check with her husband and his brother before making contact; she then apologised again, saying that she hoped the following information would be of interest, but as Terence had never come up in conversation before and as she had never met him, she'd initially thought there was very little she could share with me. However, with the help of her husband, his brother and a cousin, she was now able to pass on the little she knew. And with Jenny's help and some further research of my own, I was able to fill in some, though not all, of the gaps and finally tell Terence's story.

Terence, like his two older brothers, Richard and William, left school as soon as was legal, at the age of fourteen, possibly earlier, to work as a pony handler in the Nack[60]. Towards the end of the Second World War he joined the Territorial Army and signed up as a private in the 1st Airborne Division, working as a signalman, then as a driving and maintenance instructor.

His first military posting was to Norway in 1945 with British forces to liberate the country from five gruelling years of Nazi occupation. After the war, he'd received a certificate from the exiled King of Norway, thanking him for the part he'd played in Operation Doomsday, supervising the surrender of the German forces and preventing the sabotage of military and civilian facilities. His military reports detail a further posting to Hong Kong, describing him as trustworthy and sober with a 'good power of command'.

After the war, Terence stayed in the forces. In 1947, aged twenty-three, he married Elizabeth MacIntosh, a waitress at one of the two British Restaurants that had been set up in Seaham as part of the government's wartime communal feeding programme. Elizabeth's father, Sidney, a labourer working in one of the brick kilns on the Sunderland to Stockton turnpike, was present at the marriage ceremony at Durham Eastern Register Office on 8 February, but Terence's father, William, the coal miner, was already dead: he'd died twenty years earlier at the age of forty when Terence was only four. Small wonder the children's education had been cut so brutally short.

Terence and Elizabeth lived in Seaham and had two sons: Sid, in 1948, and Gordon, in 1950. Three years later, when Sid was five, Terence and Elizabeth separated and then divorced. Elizabeth married again and moved with the boys to King's Lynn in Norfolk, settling there and having three more children with her new husband.

The Marrin family began to drift apart and life moved on. Army papers indicated that Terence's military service terminated in October 1961, but by then, he'd already left Seaham and moved to Newcastle, where he was said to be working as a taxi driver. Sid saw his father for the last time in 1964, when he was sixteen years old, his father forty-one.

Terence joined a travelling wrestling show as a sidesman: television had revolutionised the sport's showmanship and gimmickry, and live touring shows, featuring stars like Count Bartelli, Big Daddy, Mick McManus and King Kong Kirk, were in huge demand in the mid-sixties. Terence travelled all over the country, losing touch with friends and family, who next heard from him in 1966, when he called from London to tell them of his second marriage to a Martha Raby McCue, the daughter of a Glaswegian dock worker, at a register office in Stepney, east London.

Martha and Terence lived in a dingy ground-floor flat in a dilapidated terraced building in Rampart Street, Whitechapel, in London's impoverished East End. Terence gave up the wrestling shows, found work as a fish porter at the Billingsgate Market at nearby Canary Wharf and became a father again at the age of forty-four. The baby boy was born at home in May 1967; news of the birth made it back to Seaham, but no one ever met the child.

Eleven more years passed. In 1978, Terence's sister Isabelle contacted him to say that their sister Stella was dying, and he made the long, sad journey north to Sunderland to say goodbye. By now, Martha and Terence had moved to a high-rise block of flats next to the bus station in Stockwell, south London. Terence was working as a labourer and driver but Martha was apparently already unwell.

Always close to her brother, Isabelle might have noticed a change in Terence. She certainly begged him to return home, at least to stay in touch, but despite her pleas he returned to London and it was the last anyone heard or saw of him. Tragically, Martha died in June that year, aged only fifty-one, leaving Terence behind.

Another ten years passed. In November 1987, six weeks after the storm, Isabelle, by now his only remaining sibling, learned of her brother's death only when police eventually managed to track her down. She had not seen or heard of her nephews, Sid and Gordon, for many years, but knew that she must now try to find them. On 4 December 1987, she launched an appeal in the *Sunderland Echo*:

BROTHER DIED IN OCTOBER HURRICANE
LATE NEWS ADDS TO SISTER'S LIFE OF TRAGEDY

Tragic Sunderland woman Isabelle Svenson was today in a state of shock after just discovering her brother has been crushed to death –

six weeks ago. Now Isabelle is the only remaining child out of six, the other five having all died in tragic circumstances. The latest to die was her brother Terry Marrin (64), killed by a falling tree in October's ferocious storms in London. Today Isabelle, who has launched a search to find her brother's two surviving sons, said, 'My life has been a tragedy.' Isabelle (62) of Wareness Street, Pallion, had lost touch with her brother and had not seen him for nine years. She knew he was living in London and now police have told her he was out walking with a friend in a park when a tree crashed down on him. But because he had no identification, police faced a serious problem locating relatives and it was only this week they tracked down Isabelle. Unfortunately, her brother's funeral has already been held, although she has been told his inquest is due to be held next week. Today Isabelle said she last saw her brother when he came to Wearside because one of his sisters was seriously ill. She suggested he move up to Sunderland to be near his family but although he promised to be in touch she never heard from him again. She said, 'We just drifted apart. News of his death has come as a shock and it makes it worse that it happened so long ago. The problem was he had no identification on him, but the police have been marvellous.' Isabelle's two sisters died tragically of illness, one brother died in the pit and another was killed in a hit-and-run accident in Australia. She hopes someone remembers her brother Terry, a wartime former paratrooper, from his days in Seaham and may know where his two sons Sidney and Gordon are. Anyone with information can ring her on Wearside 5675400.

After the inquest, a short news item in the *Sunderland Echo* added another remarkable dimension to Terence's story:

MAN DIED IN STORM HAVOC

Heroic Seaham man, Leo Manning, was crushed to death by a tree branch while trying to save a friend's life during ferocious storms in London. Mr Manning (64), also known as Terry Marrin, and his friend Thomas Mayor were sleeping rough in Lincoln's Inn Fields when high winds brought branches crashing down around them. St Pancras coroner, Dr Douglas Chambers, said Mr Mayor was convinced his friend tried to prevent him being crushed. Mr Marrin was the fifth of six Wearside brothers and sisters to die tragically.

Rough-sleeping figures rose dramatically between 1979 and 1990, the eleven years of Margaret Thatcher's premiership. Restrictions were placed on benefit claimants and on payments to young people, old-style hostels were shut down and, increasingly, vulnerable people found themselves homeless. Nowhere did that become more visible than in the windswept undercroft at the Queen Elizabeth Hall on the South Bank and in Lincoln's Inn Fields on the other side of the river, where bewigged barristers, and surgeons on their way to the Royal College on the north side of the square, were obliged to brush shoulders with men and women trapped in the desperate cycle of poverty, addiction and crime.

As a young outreach worker, in 1987, for the homelessness charity Thames Reach, Jeremy Swain, now that organisation's chief executive, remembered the bleak scene in the London park. Many of those living in Lincoln's Inn Fields had been there for months, some for years, and with assaults and robberies on the rise, the park had become a no-go area for the public. It was a sinister and aggressive site: the inhabitants were a static group of about eighty people living in 'bashes', surprisingly well insulated but jerry-built structures made with offcuts of wood and metal, salvaged strips of plastic, old blankets and flattened cardboard. There were fires, regular fights and disputes over drugs and alcohol.

Some of the rough sleepers had jobs, but the work was

inevitably unreliable, menial and monotonous: road sweeper, kitchen porter. Most simply tracked the soup runs during the day and gathered underneath the frail bandstand at night, resistant to the regular offers of a hostel bed, choosing to stay on the streets, even if it meant enduring freezing temperatures or, as was the case on 15 October 1987, sleeping outside in gale-force winds and heavy rain.

Jeremy was on familiar terms with the rough sleepers and thought he knew them all, but when Terence's body was recovered on the night of the storm, to his consternation and that of his colleagues, nobody knew who he was. It was possible that Terence had only recently arrived at Lincoln's Inn Fields for he was certainly not a long-term resident and had not made himself known to outreach workers at the time of his death.

Though too late for Terence, the issue of rough sleeping in Lincoln's Inn Fields came to a head at the end of the 1980s when Camden Council introduced a by-law preventing the homeless from congregating to sleep in the park. In return, it offered permanent accommodation for every rough sleeper, and Lincoln's Inn Fields was finally restored to the public.

In the last ten years, Jeremy told me, the profile of a rough sleeper has changed: as the proportion of British rough sleepers continues to fall, more than half of those on the streets of Greater London are now from Central and Eastern Europe and other countries. They are often economic migrants who have fallen foul of benefit challenges, employment and housing shortages.

The cardboard cities may have gone, the emphasis now on helping rough sleepers into accommodation, hostels, the private rented sector and treatment centres, and on helping those from abroad to reconnect with their families and return to their home countries, but mental-health problems, alcohol and addiction are still significant factors. The increased use of highly addictive and damaging psychoactive drugs, readily available on the streets, is presenting outreach workers and agencies with drastic new challenges.

Homelessness today is driven by the same things it always was: poverty, debt, addiction, relationship breakdown and mental-health problems. Men and women who have been in the services or in prison can often feel cut adrift and unable to cope when they leave those institutions and, with a lack of affordable housing, the numbers on the streets in the second decade of the twenty-first century are higher than ever.

Knowing the little I did about Terence, his impoverished childhood, his service career, his broken relationships, his move away from family and his loss of Martha, I can understand now that any one of these may have tipped him into a life on the streets.

I felt that I'd come as far as I could. Whatever else Terence had done or been, I had discovered him to be a husband and a father, a loving brother, an exemplary soldier and, at the end, a heroic friend. Perhaps now it was time to let him rest.

The sun's glare was deceptive, the northern air piercingly cold and my teeth were beginning to chatter. I turned, rubbed my arms and walked slowly along the seafront, back to the car. My journey and my year-long quest for Terence were at an end and now I wanted to be somewhere different, somewhere unconnected with the Great Storm of 1987.

I had an urge to drive north of the Tyne, to the wild empty eastern seaboard, where castles stand high above the flattened landscape and the retreating tide exposes broad miles of ridged and furrowed amber sands, so that I could stand on a beach, draw a line and move on.

I drove out of town and headed west along Lord Byron's

Walk, named for the brief and unhappy year of marriage that the poet had endured at Seaham Hall,[61] then to Sunderland, Whitley Bay and beyond. I left the A1 at Alnwick and turned towards the coast, the road bound by cropped birch hedges, claret-tipped in the low sunlight, by pale ironstone houses, ploughed fields and long-faced sheep, their backs turned on the easterly wind. After hooking right to Embleton Bay, for a glimpse of ruined Dunstanburgh, rising from a dolerite ridge and surrounded on three sides by the sea, I turned north again to Beadnell, where wild ponies grazed on grass-topped dunes. At the coastal town of Seahouses, I parked and left the car to stretch my legs.

From here, boats with names like *St Cuthbert II* and *Glad Tidings III* take twitchers and day-trippers on tours around the nearby Farne Islands, where grey seals and puffins share the rocky outcrops with fulmars, kittiwakes and terns in their thousands, and green-eyed shags nest in shrieking colonies on the clifftops. But the boats don't sail in winter: they'd all been raised on trestles for their annual service and only a few cobles,[62] hung with brightly coloured floats, rocked at their moorings in the harbour.

The surface of the water in the empty dock was skittish, the cloud-whipped sky prophetic. I walked back to the car, left Seahouses behind, drove on past clapboard houses, dune-fringed beaches and the imposing castle stronghold at Bamburgh, spectacular in the fading afternoon light, for the final few miles to Lindisfarne.

The roads were empty now. An icy breeze had dispatched the sun and a dark snow cloud broke over the horizon, its deconstructed edge like spoiled spooled wool. I'd arrived too late to make the crossing and the low causeway to the Holy Isle was impassable, white lines on the asphalt disappearing into a tidal scoop, long shore grass drowned, yet still waving in the yellowing half-light. Only the old ash poles, water-worn sentinels, stood to honour where the road should have been, between the mainland and the mysterious island, a long, low, medieval mass in the distance.

I stood at the waterline, lifted my face to the sacred sky and allowed snowflakes to surprise my lashes. My tired mind floundered with drifting images of storms and slag heaps, ferries, tugs and fishing boats in mountainous seas, fallen trees and apple trees, sailors and fishermen, wet cardboard boxes, pearl earrings, pithead wheels and filthy-faced men, hauled to the earth's surface in a steel crate, their wide eyes as white as the wave tops in the narrow channel between me and the hallowed up-thrust of igneous rock in the distance.

The deep well of sadness at my father's death would never leave me, but the storm, the mural and this windblown journey had allowed me to understand and celebrate the person he was and everything he'd left behind. Comforted now, and calm, I breathed deeply and turned away from the water's edge. I felt the coal dust in my hair, tasted sea salt on my lips, thanked Fate, fortune, family and the serendipitous twists of time and place that make us who we are.

Epilogue

SPRING

2017

paint me into your landscape,
let me stay with you

Springtime in Kew: pavement cherry trees a confection of pink; smart townhouse balconies buckling under the woody weight of contorted wisteria stems, fat buds about to burst into purple flower. On Kew Green, handsome in sunlight, Hunter House, with its high, silent galleries, its labelled lockers groaning with pressed, dried and preserved plant samples, bequeathed to the Herbarium by hunters and heroes: by Wilson and Hooker, Livingstone and Darwin, brought to Kew from all corners of the globe. From the jungle swamps of Lao Cai, and the Chinese provinces of Hubei and Sichuan, from Darjeeling and Sikkim, from the Zambezi River and the volcanic islands of the Galapagos.

I enter the Gardens through the Elizabeth Gate, walk the wide asphalt pathways past the luminous Nash Conservatory, up to the Orangery, and down the formal Broad Walk towards the lake, where tourists pose for selfies beside a recklessly-previous magnolia or before of one of Princess Augusta's gnarly, all-knowing, 300-year-old Lions.

For the most part, the arboretum is still waiting to green; many of the trees still pencil-sketched geometries against the boyish-blue sky. A thousand of them, planted as saplings straight after the storm – couched in shallow pits and circled with mulch on Kew's sand and gravel river terraces – are young adults now, already moving into the next phase of growth and maturity, though none will reach their prime in my lifetime. For each individual shape, stem and seed, for every branch, bark and bud – a name, a kingdom, a botanical significance, a story.

In the tea room at Victoria Gate, I cast around for my children, young adults now, too. I see them, all three, standing together in front of the Kew Mural where we've agreed to meet. Hands in pockets or on hips, heads tilted to one side, identical sandy brows in their trademark, contemplative furrow.

I hold back for a moment, observe their shared height, frame, hair colour, expressions and stance; register the complex but unmistakeable generational legacies; identify fleeting traces of succession and survival. And I know that what they've been given is just the start: that each of them will have the chance to tell their own story, in their own way – and all in good time.

Appendix 1

THE HERALD OF FREE ENTERPRISE

March 1987

At 1905 hours on 6 March 1987, the *Herald of Free Enterprise*, a Townsend Thoresen roll-on roll-off ferry, left the port of Zeebrugge on its way to Dover carrying 459 passengers, 80 crew, 81 cars, 3 buses and 47 trucks. Among the passengers were army personnel returning home from German bases, families, holidaymakers and groups of friends. Many were day-trippers who had taken advantage of a promotion in the *Sun* newspaper for a cheap visit to the continent, collecting tokens and sending them off with a pound note to get their complimentary ferry tickets. They'd crossed the Channel in the morning, spent the day sightseeing, shopping and visiting the bars of Zeebrugge and, after boarding the ferry at six o' clock, were congregating in the cafés, duty-free shops and viewing lounges for the four-and-a-half-hour journey home. The early evening sea was cold but calm, and a light breeze was blowing from the south-east.

The *Herald* had not been designed with the port of Zeebrugge in mind: the ramp, or 'linkspan', by which vehicles were loaded onto the upper car deck (and which for the berths at Calais was the correct height), could not be raised high enough at Zeebrugge. To compensate, the vessel's bow ballast tanks needed to be filled with water or 'trimmed', lowering the ship deeper into the sea to allow the harbour ramps to operate correctly, and for vehicles to board. When the *Herald* sailed out of

Zeebrugge harbour at 1905 hours on 6 March, not all that water had been pumped back out of the ballast tanks and the ship was still three feet down at the bow.

There were huge pairs of doors at both ends, bow and stern, that closed like clam shells, flush to the ship's hull, and the usual safe practice was to close both sets of doors before sailing, a procedure that took approximately four minutes. On the night of 6 March, however, although the stern doors had been shut, the crew member responsible for closing the bow doors had fallen asleep in his cabin and nobody else had thought to check or close them in his absence. If you had been on the ship that night, standing on the car deck looking out of the bow doors before sailing, you would have seen the sea at precisely the same level as the deck, water lapping at the doors' edge.

With her bow doors open and the ballast tanks full, making her sit lower in the water than usual, the *Herald* backed out of her berth at 1905 that night, five minutes behind schedule. The captain stepped outside the bridge momentarily to watch astern as the ferry moved away from her mooring, but as he had no way of checking the status of the bow doors from that position, and there were no lights on his control panel to show whether they had been shut or not, the ship was allowed to sail on, with rapid and tragic consequences.

The harbour tug towed the *Herald* from the inner harbour towards the Kennedy Quay at a speed of five knots; once the tow had been dropped, she quickened, passing the outer mole at 1924 when the captain increased the speed again from 14 to 18 knots. With this sharp change in speed and still in comparatively shallow waters, the height of the forward wave dragged the bow of the ship down and sea water began to pour through the gaping doors onto the car deck, slopping and swirling around the tyres of the vehicles parked inside.

The stability of a ship like the *Herald* depends on a constant centre of gravity, but if there is an uncontrolled mass, like seawater, moving inside the vessel, the centre of gravity will inevitably shift with the ship's every heave and roll. Within seconds of passing the outer mole, and with thousands of gallons of water now swilling across the lower deck, the ship began to list 30 degrees to port, righting herself briefly as the water sloshed to starboard, then listing again to port as the seawater rolled heavily back. With water flowing into the ship through the bow doors at a rate of 200 tons per minute, there was no longer any chance for her to recover and she tipped, fatally, to one side. Within ninety seconds she had turned 180 degrees to starboard and capsized portside in the freezing Belgian waters. She settled on a sandbank 0.7 nautical miles from the harbour entrance, facing back the way she'd come, half filled with water, her electrical systems immediately destroyed, her walkways, bars, cafeterias, kiosks, cabins and everyone within them plunged into horrifying darkness.

As the ship settled on the sea bed, some lucky passengers managed to escape and some were rescued, thanks to the swift action of the Belgian Navy, but many more were trapped deep inside the groaning vessel, cold and terrified, treading water in the frigid darkness. The rescue effort was now a race against the tide, but eventually the rising sea made it impossible to continue and the last of those left alive inside the ship died of drowning and hypothermia in water that was barely above freezing.

Only sixty-one of the victims were recovered from the wreck on the night of the sinking, leaving many dead inside, but the operation to recover the remaining bodies could not take place for another month until the wreck had been made stable. A mammoth salvage was planned and a complex lifting operation, involving sheerlegs and pull barges, designed to lift the 7,950-ton *Herald* into a level position above the waterline.

Once she was righted, Royal Navy divers recovered 123 bodies
from the wreck, many of them remarkably well preserved by
the thick slime of the sea bed. Divers eventually recovered
the final bodies, and bulldozers cleared the silted car decks
of their mangled payload. On 13 May the ship was towed to
Vlissingen in Holland where, battered and corroded, she
skulked out of sight for another three months while Townsend
Thoresen decided what to do with her.

In Vlissingen, the *Herald* was declared a total loss and put
up for sale; there were, unsurprisingly, few takers. She had been
in service for only seven years, which in the life of a ship is
no time at all. Despite her ordeal, she was still afloat, still
structurally sound and eminently salvageable, but she was a
liability: no member of the public would knowingly board her,
and it would be hard to find seamen willing to sail in her.
Townsend Thoresen sold her to the Jamaican shipping company
Compania Naviera SA at the end of September 1987. They
slapped a cursory layer of white over her signage, giving her
a new name, *Flushing Range*. The distinctive TT logos on the
crumpled blue funnels were also camouflaged and the plan to
tow her to Taiwan for scrap swung into action.

It's rumoured that the *Herald of Free Enterprise* may never have
been scrapped at all: even thirty years after the accident, stories
still circulate, in maritime circles, that she was seen being towed
from the Taiwanese breakers to a separate dock in Kaohsiung,
where she was allegedly repaired, refurbished and refloated
under a different name: that she still operates as a passenger
ferry, somewhere in the world, today.

Appendix 2

ASYLUM SEEKERS

Fortunately for the Tamils and for all genuine asylum-seekers in the UK, their interests were to be represented in court by the immigration lawyer David Burgess, whose legal-aid firm Winstanley-Burgess specialised in asylum work at a time when immigration law was in its infancy.

David Burgess's tenacity, dedication and compassion for his embattled clients had already resulted in several trailblazing legal successes when the large group of Tamils had arrived. After they were threatened with immediate return to Sri Lanka, it was David Burgess who intervened on their behalf, using the only statutory option available through the courts at that time: a judicial review of the decision to send them all home.

Court proceedings can be slow and cumbersome, judicial reviews more so than most, but in the UK, at the time, there were simply no other legal mechanisms for a rejected asylum-seeker to appeal against repatriation. A raft of legal and policy changes had been introduced in the months before the storm to limit the numbers arriving and seeking asylum in the UK and, having many applications to deal with, the government selected six of the Tamils as test cases.

Although the violent civil war in Sri Lanka was still ongoing and although lawyers, Amnesty International, the British Refugee Council and the United Nations High Commissioner for Refugees (UNHCR) all urged the government not to send the Tamils back because of the instability, the known human-rights violations and the targeting of young male Tamils in particular, judgement was issued against them in the House of Lords in December 1987: it was asserted that the men would not face persecution in Sri Lanka just because they were Tamils.

The men were sent back. Several were detained and tortured; one man reported that he was quickly arrested by government forces, accused of being a member of the rebel group, the Tamil Tigers, interrogated, stripped and beaten with iron bars and sand-filled PVC pipes, subjected to electric-shock treatment to his genitals, tied upside down and a fire lit with chillies underneath his head until he passed out.

David Burgess had no intention of abandoning these men: funding rarely stopped him doing what he thought legally and morally right. In an unprecedented move, he travelled to Sri Lanka, accompanied by his young assistant, solicitor Chris Randall, traced the men and collected evidence of their persecution, *pro bono*, to mount out-of-country asylum appeals on their behalf. After further hearings in the UK, the men were given leave to return, as refugees, while their cases were argued further. Known as Vilvarajah and Others v. The United Kingdom, the case reached the European Court of Human Rights in 1991, where judges recognised judicial review as an inadequate and inappropriate means of challenging refusal of entry. Although the case was lost, it would eventually lead to a dramatic change in the law that gives all rejected asylum-seekers the right to appeal without having to return to their home country first.

By the time the case ended, conditions had once again worsened in Sri Lanka and many of the original cohort of Tamil refugees, including the men represented by David and Chris, remained in the UK, but what David called the government's 'street-fighting approach' to refugee litigation continued. In an article for the *New Law Journal* in 1991, he criticised the government for actively engaging in 'undermining refugee protection' and described how the prevailing governmental attitude towards migrants and asylum-seekers had filtered down to front-line immigration officials at UK airports, whose treatment of new arrivals was often cruel and dismissive. 'Government has yet to demonstrate any great concern that asylum-seekers have been rendered the target of abusive and inhuman behaviour,'[63] he wrote.

At sixty-three years old, David Burgess was pushed to his death under a Tube train at King's Cross station by a client, a young Sri Lankan man. The shock and manner of his untimely loss is still felt keenly by his former colleague Chris Randall, and by many other people whose lives were changed by working with a man so uniquely talented and humane. Chris was asked by a legal publication to write a tribute to his former mentor and friend in which he movingly describes David's legacy, his many legal achievements as well as the human qualities – the fearlessness, dedication, compassion and humility – that made him 'the finest immigration solicitor of his generation'.

Appendix 3

A TRIBUTE TO DAVID BURGESS

By Chris Randall

David Burgess, who was the finest immigration solicitor of his generation, and inspired two generations of younger immigration and human rights practitioners, myself included, has died suddenly. David, who was latterly also known and lived as Sonia Burgess, was a long-standing ILPA member who attended the founding meeting of the organisation in 1984.

David was already very active in the newly developing field of immigration law when in 1985 I was recruited to Winstanley-Burgess, the legal-aid firm he had helped found a few years earlier. I was his trainee from 1985 to 1987, his employee from 1987 to 1990, and one of his partners from 1990 until we closed the firm in 2003. For me, as for many others, working with him was life-changing.

His legal achievements are extraordinary, but have been chronicled elsewhere; see in particular, the excellent obituary by Fiona Bawdon in the *Guardian* at http://www.guardian.co.uk/law/2010/nov/02/david-burgess-obituary. In short, though, he was centrally involved in many of the leading immigration cases of the 1980s and 1990s. He acted in the first two Refugee Convention cases to reach the House of Lords; in the subsequent application by Sivakumaran and others to the ECHR (which, although unsuccessful, precipitated the introduction of an in-country right of appeal for asylum-seekers); in the ground-breaking cases of Chahal, which, in establishing the inviolable nature of Article 3 ECHR protection, created a bastion that still protects migrants today; and of M, a successful attempt to bring contempt proceedings against a minister of the Crown. That list alone merits high praise; but it is not the whole story.

Those who worked with David know that the same extraordinary level of dedication and care, which Nick Blake has described in respect of David's work in the Chahal case, went into every case he did, whatever the profile of the client, and even if no big constitutional issue was at stake. The interests of the client (usually a migrant but often another kind of outsider) were always absolutely at the centre of his work. In many ways he was something of an outsider himself: his was a position of empathy with the client, not sympathy; he did not do 'professional detachment'. He drove himself extremely hard, probably too hard, and those working with him, whether solicitors, barristers, caseworkers, interpreters or experts, were inspired to do the same. In spite of that personal cost, I have no doubt that many of us who worked with him over the years look back at those times and know that it was with him, or inspired by him, and certainly because of him, that our best work was done. Perhaps because of this client-centred approach, he reserved particular opprobrium for legal representatives who let their clients down with poor-quality work – sadly too large a group.

It is also not surprising that David helped create at Winstanley-Burgess a unique environment, for workers and clients alike. The office was fairly basic, but rarely closed; many of the support staff worked loyally there for over a decade. After his death, one staff member recalled David providing food for hungry clients; and a long-standing interpreter said how casual staff adopted the office as their unofficial workplace. Great

commitment was demanded; but advisors were given responsibility early, and many blossomed.

David also inspired great client loyalty; the messages from all
quarters on his death bear witness to that. I well recall that two
of the Tamils who returned to the UK with Mr Sivakumaran
would come and see us every year for over a decade after their
case was finished. Similarly, he was well known and respected
for his work with people from the Tibetan, Sikh, Tamil, Philippine
and Kurdish communities. He acted for many individuals from
those communities – but his cases helped many more people.
Not surprisingly a number of his clients were inspired themselves
to become lawyers. He was also much respected by and consulted
by a very wide range of organisations, working closely with the
Medical Foundation, Refugee Arrivals Project, Refugee Legal
Centre and Press for Change to name just a few.

David showed a unique imagination in how he ran cases – in
1988, at his suggestion, he and I followed Mr Sivakumaran and
his compatriots, following their defeat in the House of Lords,
back to Sri Lanka to collect evidence to mount (*pro bono*)
out-of-country asylum appeals for the men, something which
had rarely been tried, yet which, by its success showed better
than any academic article the ineffectiveness of judicial review
as the standard remedy for refused port asylum applicants. The
introduction of a proper appeal right for asylum-seekers has
its genesis in this case. Later, working closely with voluntary
and community organisations, he inspired similar ground-
breaking work in Turkey, when, with the imposition of visas
looming, British immigration officers were encouraging airlines
not to allow would-be asylum-seekers to board planes to the
UK, were preventing them from lodging claims when they
arrived, and were summarily removing them. As a result of
evidence gathered in Turkey, significant numbers were returned
to be given access to the UK's asylum procedures.

It will come as no surprise that funding issues rarely prevented David from adopting a legal tactic that he thought was the right legal and moral way forward in a case, and that he did very significant amounts of *pro bono* work. However, his legal work was not restricted to immigration. He also undertook, or helped in, a number of important transgender cases, over the years, which reflected his deep and growing personal interest in those issues. As usual, his energy was unbounded.

Yet in spite all these achievements David was an extremely humble person – that indeed was the source of his deep respect for his clients. I don't think he ever stood for elected office, and he rarely spoke in public, or wrote articles. He was the first to leave a social gathering, particularly of lawyers, if he attended at all. However, when he did publish something, or make a speech, he prepared minutely and for that reason was all the more effective. No one who was there will forget the mauling he inflicted on one particular head of the Legal Services Commission at the ILPA conference in 2003, speaking for all of us as he did it. One of his most public statements of his concerns about poor-quality legal representation was in a rare *New Law Journal* article in 1997 entitled 'Legal representation can kill' (http://www.allwomencount.net/EWC%20LAW/Asylum/LegalRepresentationCanKill.htm) where he wrote of a client that

> As an asylum seeker S was more failed than most. She was failed by the Home Office, by the Courts but above all by her representatives. In the field of asylum work it is a truth known to practitioners that legal representation can kill.

Perhaps because of his humility, David struggled over the years with the role of a 'radical lawyer' and, indeed, with his role as a provider of publicly funded legal services through a small business. He was never a member of even the 'alternative' legal establishment. He, the most co-operative of workers, worried more and more about the competitiveness that can exist in our sector, even though few would have begrudged him the pick of the most exciting cases. I particularly recall, during the Pinochet extradition episode, his typically searching self-examination over what was motivating him to do particular pieces of work; in the end he withdrew from the case, offered his work to other parties, and to my mind was never again at ease with the role of a trail-blazing lawyer. It is also entirely consistent with his approach to life that he would be far harder on himself in these moments than anyone else would have been.

Perhaps these growing concerns were a blessing in disguise for him, and perhaps they were what David needed to move on to concentrate on other important aspects of his life. He decided to leave Winstanley-Burgess in 2003; and in the end the remaining partners decided to close the firm, unable to see a future that did not involve even longer hours, or serried ranks of case-workers. After that I saw less of him, as he initially studied Tibetan at the University in Lhasa, in preparation for working there alongside his wife, a plan he was in the end forced to change. He had for many years had issues about his own gender identity, as many of his closer friends and his loving family knew. Perhaps because he was now freed from the restrictions of professional life, he started to live increasingly in the identity of Sonia, rather than David, Burgess, although when he returned to more low-profile professional work, latterly with the Medical Foundation and Luqmani Thomson, he continued to be known as David. Those of us who knew less about this part of his life were heartened at a moving vigil held for him at his church of St Martin-in-the-Fields to find that he was as loved, valued and respected as Sonia by his friends there, as he was as David by us, and that of course Sonia showed in her participation there her familiar humility and concern for others, many of whom had no idea of her illustrious legal background. Those who knew him best have said that he was happier living as Sonia, which will be a comfort for all of us as we come to terms with our loss. We can speculate as to whether he enjoyed the way that he compartmentalised elements of his life, or whether that was just the only defence he had against a world that does not cope well with individuality such as his. Either way, we immigration lawyers, along with many other communities and institutions, have lost a giant from amongst us, and have been deprived of the opportunity to tell David/Sonia that before she left us.

This tribute first appeared in the mailing of the Immigration Law Practitioners Association (ILPA) 2011

Appendix 4

THE EARL WILLIAM

The hundreds of yachts and small boats that moor at Chaguaramas on the north-west coast of Trinidad come to sail the gentle waters of the Gulf of Paria, a shallow inland sea that lies between this most southern Caribbean island and the eastern coast of Venezuela.

To the north, the gulf is connected to the Caribbean through the Bocas del Dragón, or dragon's mouths, blue-green sailways that separate five idyllic tropical offshore islands: Chacachacare, Monos, Gasparee, Huevos and Centipede. Lush vegetation drapes over steep cliffs that drop down to the water's edge, while in secret island coves and on secluded beaches, motor boats launch from the private jetties of clapboard houses, immaculately painted in lemon yellow and palest pink – the second and third homes of the very rich.

In 1498 when Columbus discovered Trinidad and the Venezuelan mainland, he named the Gulf the Golfo de la Ballena, for the whales that came to calve in its gentle waters, but once colonial whaling stations were established here in the eighteenth century, the whales didn't stand a chance. Within sixty years the whole population been hunted, harpooned and hacked to extinction, their blubber sliced and boiled in vast sugar coppers to extract the precious oil.

These days, there's no sign of whales: the waters in the Gulf are plundered for shrimp and finfish instead, and countless rigs, both floating and fixed, drill day and night for oil and natural gas in Trinidad's deep hydrocarbon basins. The islands and their surrounding waters are now the offshore pleasure grounds of yachtsmen, and the hundreds of Caribbean party boats that leave the harbour at midnight and return with their bleary-eyed passengers at dawn.

In September 2007, twenty years after hurricane winds had battered the English coastline in the Great Storm and thousands of miles away, Basil Joseph, Trinidadian sailor, entrepreneur and chairman of Chaguaramas' most profitable party-boat business, Treasure Queen Tours, proudly unveiled his latest maritime venture: *Ocean Pearl*, a five-star luxury floating hotel, moored at Williams Bay, Chaguaramas. Liveried in the Trinidian national colours, with a large painted steelpan at the stern, the ship had undergone a $30 million refit and now boasted a vast conference hall, sixty-three luxury cabins, a fine-dining restaurant serving seafood and steaks, and several bars over its seven decks.

'We decided to try this venture,' said the ebullient Captain Joseph, 'because we realised there was a need for a place like this, where people could party and enjoy themselves in a safe environment, with a place to stay overnight if they were too tired to drive home afterward.' He went on to stress that *Ocean Pearl* had been stripped of its engines and would not sail from port, declaring, with no hint of irony, 'She is in permanent anchor here at Chaguaramas and is capable of withstanding hurricanes, as is.'

Captain Joseph would have known, of course, that *Ocean Pearl* had already had a very long life at sea. She hadn't looked so good in years, certainly never as glamorous. Since launching for the first time from the Norwegian shipyards in 1964, she'd been sold and resold, renamed and repainted in a variety of different liveries; she'd worked the Irish Sea and the Mediterranean, sailed from southern Italy to Greece, been chartered around Malta, Jamaica and the Windward Islands, and laid up in Falmouth, Milford Haven, Bari and Trinidad.

As *Earl William*, owned by British Rail and operated by Sealink, she'd sailed from Dover to Calais and from Southampton to Cherbourg and the Channel Islands. In 1987, in perhaps her most ignoble incarnation, she'd been commandeered by the British Home Office, converted to an immigrant detention centre hosting a hundred asylum-seekers in the English port of Harwich. She'd collided with a beacon in Jersey and a petrol tanker in Port of Spain, been repaired both times and put back to work. Since 2004, she'd been moored and abandoned in the Gulf of Paria, a yawning, rusting, malodorous hulk.

What a million-dollar Caribbean contrast for the *Earl William* to be reinvented as a static, five-star 'floatel' after so many years' relentless hard work.

At dawn on the morning of 2 April 2011, *Ocean Pearl* was under tow to the tugboat *Icon 1*, moving slowly north and east of her mooring in Chaguaramas Harbour to a new berth in Puerto Sucre, Venezuela. In choppy waters in the half-dark, first the tug and then the garishly painted dead ship struck the starboard bow of a static drill ship *PetroSaudi Saturn*, severing two of the eight mooring lines that kept the ship at her drilling site.

Instantly and dangerously destabilised, *PetroSaudi Saturn* drifted rapidly, her 200-ton hydraulic hoisting gear roughly hauled up from the oil wellhead 480 feet below the ship and left lying across the surface of the water at an angle of 22.5 degrees. Fatally holed by the *Saturn*'s mooring wires, *Ocean Pearl* had sunk without trace by the time the sun came up.

The oil well was abandoned, the newly refitted *Ocean Pearl* lost to the deep, and when *PetroSaudi Saturn*'s reparation was added, insurance costs for this one incident amounted to a record $100 million.

Even in a year with an unprecedented series of natural disasters, including earthquakes in Japan and New Zealand, hurricanes in the US and floods in Thailand and Australia, the accident in the Caribbean still amounted to Lloyds' second biggest payout of 2011.

ACKNOWLEDGEMENTS

Thanks to family and friends who helped me with this book and to my many interviewees, who so generously shared their wisdom and their memories.

At Kew, I am particularly grateful to Tony Kirkham, also to Mark Nesbitt and Frances Cook in the Economic Botany Collection, to Peter Gasson in the Joddrell Laboratory, to the staff in the Library, Art and Archives, and at Wakehurst, to Iain Parkinson and Sandra Howard. Special thanks to Robert Games, to John Makepeace and to Lisa Pearson at the Library of the Arnold Arboretum at Harvard.

I am greatly indebted to Ray Hawes of the National Trust, a very busy man who made time for me and showed such enthusiasm for this project; to Chris Heels and to the extraordinarily helpful people in the National Trust press office. Thanks to Tony Whitbread and Amanda Reeves of the Sussex Wildlife Trust, and to David Russell, whose testimony made such an impact on me.

Sincere and grateful thanks to the forecaster Peter Gibbs, whose effortless explanations made complex meteorology very clear, and to Mark Beswick and Duncan Ball at the Met Office. Thanks to Gerry Douglas Sherwood, for allowing me to quote from his lighthouse diaries; to Peter Coglan in Hastings; to the luthiers, Stephen Barber and Sandi Harris and to the English apple men and women, Helen Brent-Smith, Sandys Dawes, John Guest, Dave Kaspar and Charles Tassell.

It was a privilege to talk to the humanitarian, Martin Barber, and to Chris Randall, who shared his personal memories and allowed me to reproduce his moving tribute to David Burgess. Thanks also to David Horn and David Whittle in Harwich. For teaching me all about tugboats and giving me a great day on the water, thanks to Captain Paul Thomas, John Burgess, Sandy Finlay, Emma Gilbrook, Ben Pearce, Scott Pritchard, Gary Rawlings and everyone at the Fowey Harbour Office.

I would like to say a very special thank you to Jenny, Sid and Gordon Marrin for letting me tell Terence's story; to Jeremy Swain of Thames Reach and his remarkable colleagues, especially Isobel McKenna and Sam Perry and to Julie Taylor at St Pancras Coroners Court.

Many thanks to Jan Fortune, to the poet, Caroline Davies and to the dedicated team at Cinnamon Press, whose commitment and enthusiasm gave me the confidence to embark on this project in the first place.

To my guide and champion, James Long, to Margaret Brereton, Marion Milne and to the one and only Viv Groskop, thank you; what it is to have friends like you. Huge thanks to my irrepressible agent, Cathryn Summerhayes at Curtis Brown, who took the idea and ran with it, and to my editor, Rupert Lancaster, whose calm ingenuity and vision have transformed this book.

To Hazel Orme, for her exquisite attention to detail, to Ben Summers for his striking cover design, to Cameron Myers, Maddy Price, Becca Mundy and to everyone at Hodder and Stoughton, thank you for your unedited enthusiasm for this book.

Windblown was first conceived as a poetry collection, inspired by the events of October 1987 as a tribute to my late father, Terry Thomas. I would not have been able to write it without the memories of my aunt, Joy Cremin, or the unconditional love and support of my mother, Joyce Thomas, and my children, Matilda, Kitty and Rufus Treverton Jones. Finally, my love and thanks to Owen McNeir, who, with insight, humour and endless patience, has walked every step of this windblown journey with me.

TTJ, June 2017

PICTURE ACKNOWLEDGEMENTS

SELECT BIBLIOGRAPHY

Aalto, Kathryn, *The Natural World of Winnie The Pooh* (Portland, Oregon, Timber Press, 2015)

Adams, Max, *The Wisdom of Trees* (London, Head of Zeus, 2014)

Barber, *Martin, Blinded by Humanity: Inside the UN's Humanitarian Operations* (London, IB Tauris and Co., London, 2016)

Bridge, M.C.; Gasson, P.E. and Cutler, D.F., 'Dendro-climatological observations on trees at Kew and Wakehurst Place: event and pointer years' (*Forestry*, Vol 69, No.3, 1996)

Briggs, Roy W., *'Chinese' Wilson: A Life of Ernest H Wilson 1876 1930* (London, HMSO, 1993)

Burgess, David, 'Asylum by Ordeal' (*New Law Journal*, Vol 141/ Issue 6487 NLJ 50, January 1991)

Coleman, David; Sisman, Richard; Potts, Don; Forsyth, Sue; Brown, Michael, *Task Force Trees Action Pack* (London, Countryside Commission, 1998)

Cutler, D.F.; Gasson, P.E.; Farmer, M.C., 'The Wind Blown Tree Root Survey: Preliminary Results' (*Arboricultural Journal*, 1989, Vol 13 pp 219–242, AB Academic Publishers, Great Britain, 1989)

Eden, Philip, *Great British Weather Disasters* (London, Continuum, 2008)

Deakin, Roger, *Waterlog*, (London, Vintage, 2000)

Defoe, Daniel, *The Storm*, (London, 2005, Penguin Books. First published 1704)

Du Pré, Hilary; Du Pré, Piers, *A Genius in the Family: An*

Intimate Portrait of Jacqueline du Pré (London, Chatto and Windus, 1997)

Fellbridge and District History Group, *Buxted Park*, http://www.felbridge.org.uk/index.php/publications/buxted-park/

Fish, Michael, MBE; McGaskill, Ian; Hudson, Paul, *Storm Force: Britain's Wildest Weather* (Ilkely, Northern, 2007)

Flanagan, Mark; Kirkham, Tony, *Plants from the Edge of the World: New Explorations in the Far East* (Portland, Oregon, Timber Press, 2005)

Flanagan, Mark; Kirkham, Tony, *Wilson's China: A Century On* (London, Kew Publishing, 2009)

Goodwin, Chris *About the Lute: A brief introduction to the Lute* http://www.lutesociety.org/pages/about-the-lute 2001

Grayson, A.J. (Ed) *The 1987 Storm: Impacts and Responses.* Chapter 5: Harvesting and Marketing the Windblown Timber. (Forestry Commission, Farnham, 1989)

Harmer, Ralph; Tucker, Nick; Nickerson, Ralph, 'Natural Regeneration in storm damaged woods – 1987 storm sites revisited' (*Quarterly Journal of Forestry*, Vol 98 No.3, July 2004, Royal Forestry Society)

Hill, George, *Hurricane Force* (London, Collins, 1988)

Hunt, Kathleen, *Wakehurst Place, Yesterday, Today and Tomorrow: The Storm of 16th October 1987* (Archives, Kew, 1987)

JOC.com 'Taiwan Ship Scrapping Firms are Heading for the Scrap Heap' (September 26, 1998) http://www.joc.com/maritime-news/taiwan-ship-scrapping-firms-are-heading-scrap-heap_19880926.html

Kirkham, Tony, 'The Decompaction Programme on Trees at Kew' (*International Dendrology Society Yearbook*, 2008)

Leopold, Aldo, *A Sand County Almanac and Sketches Here and There* (New York, Oxford University Press, 1949)

Mabey, Richard, *The Ash and The Beech: The Drama of Woodland Change* (London, Vintage, 2013)

Mabey, Richard, 'Wildwoods don't need our help to survive "apocalyptic" diseases' (FT.com, 26 June 2015)

Mayhew, Clive, 'Disappearing Avenues: Living Features in A Changing Landscape', (http://cmarb.co.uk/assets/documents/Disappearing-Avenues.pdf) 2007

Martell, Charles, *Native Apples of Gloucestershire* (Gloucestershire Orchard Trust, 2014)

Moon, A.V., 'The influx of Sabine's Gulls and other Seabirds in October 1987' (*London Bird Report* No.52 for 1987)

Musgrave, Toby; Gardner, Chris; Musgrave, Will, *The Plant Hunters: Two Hundred Years of Adventure and Discovery Around the World* (London, Ward Lock, 1998)

Navy Department, *Admiralty Manual of Seamanship:* v. 3 (Stationery Office Books, 1983)

Parker, Tony, *Lighthouse*, (London, Eland, 1975)

Pearson, Lynn F., *Lighthouses* (Oxford, Shire Publications, 1995)

Peak, Steve, *Fishermen of Hastings: 200 Years of the Hastings Fishing Community* (St Leonard's-on-Sea, Newsbooks 1985)

Rackham, Oliver, *The Ash Tree*, (Fratrum, Dorset, Little Toller, 2014)

Russell, David, *Forestry and the Art of Frying Small Fish* (Cambridge, The White Horse Press, 1998)

Russell, David, *Wild by Nature: Activating the Wild Psyche* (Ecos, 26 (1) 2005)

Russell, David, 'What Is a Wood? What Are We Doing?' (National Trust Conference, 'A millennium celebration of trees' Staverton Park 2000)

Russell, David, 'The Spiritual Dimension to the Management of Trees and Woods' (National Trust Forestry Commission)

Russell, James, *Man-made Eden* (Sansom, Bristol, 2009)

Simmons, John, 'An Arboricidal Wind' (Kew, Archives, 1987)

Thornton, Nigel; Goodfellow, Ray, 'Mv Herald of Free

Enterprise, Past and Present' (www.doverferryphotosforums.
co.uk October 2012)

Tudge, Colin, *The Secret Life of Trees: How They Live and Why
They Matter*, (London, Penguin, 2005)

Voices from the Hastings Stade (Hastings Fishermen's Museum,
2012)

Weather Magazine, Vol 43, No. 3, 1988 Special Issue, *The Storm
of 15-16 October 1987*

Whitbread, Tony, *When the Wind Blew* (Royal Society of Nature
Conservation, 1991)

Yardley, Iain, *Ninety Seconds at Zeebrugge, The Herald of Free
Enterprise Story* (Stroud, Gloucestershire, The History Press,
2014)

ENDNOTES

1. Following their defeat in the Boat Race the previous year, the Oxford team had controversially recruited several American post-graduate rowers to build the fastest possible squad. There were many disputes over the team selection and training methods of the Oxford coach, Dan Topolski, and in the build-up to the 1987 race the American contingent staged several very public walk-outs.

2. A hurricane is a rotating low pressure system with sustained winds of 74 m.p.h. that forms over the warm ocean waters of the Atlantic basin between July and October. An intense low-level build-up of heat and energy is released as it rises and meets cooler air.

3. The last weather ship in the North Atlantic, the MS *Polarfront*, stationed at Point Mike, 66°N 02°E, was finally decommissioned in 2009. With annual operational costs at €2.5 million, almost all of it paid for by the Norwegian Meteorological Institute in Oslo, the *Polarfront*, which had been deployed for more than sixty years, was using up more than half of the institute's running expenses for all meteorological observations in the country, and despite the ship's collection of valuable climate change data, in the end, the Norwegians could no longer justify her existence.

4. The World Meteorological Organization Voluntary Observing Ship scheme, by which merchant ships on the world's oceans and seas, known as ships of opportunity, are recruited and trained to take and transmit meteorological observations.

5. The Nansen bottle, a device for collecting samples of seawater at depth, was designed in 1894 by the Norwegian oceanographer and explorer Fridtjof Nansen.

6. Bathymetry was originally the measurement of ocean depth by soundings, but it has also come to include submarine topography: it examines the shape as well as the depth of underwater terrain.

7. The Decca Navigator System was a hyperbolic navigation system used by ships and aircraft to chart their position by receiving radio signals from fixed navigational beacons.

8. Kaoliang is a strong distilled liquor made from fermented sorghum. It can range from 35% to 63% alcohol by volume and is popular in China, Taiwan and Korea.

9. See appendix 1.

10. The *Iolaire* was carrying sailors who had fought in the First World War back to the Scottish island of Lewis. She left Kyle of Lochalsh on the mainland late on the evening of 31 December 1918. But, at 2.30 a.m. on New Year's Day, as the ship approached the port of Stornoway, a few yards offshore and a mile away from the safety of Stornoway Harbour, she hit the infamous Beasts of Holm and eventually sank. The final death toll was officially put at 205, of whom 181 were islanders, but as the ship was badly overcrowded and there was a lack of proper records the death toll may have been higher.

11. Derelict is the term used to describe a vessel that has abandoned its tow.

12. The Needles was the last lighthouse in the UK to retain boat relief.

13. The coal-fired Rayburn at the Needles lighthouse was maintained and run until the final days before full automation.

14. The term breeches buoy – essentially a canvas seat with a float attached – is the literal description for a rope-based rescue method used in dangerous situations at sea or for transferring people from one location to another over water.

15. A deadship is one in which the engines and boilers are not in operation due to the absence of power.

16. Hansard, 17 February 1987 Vol 110 cc 769–74

17. Hansard, 3 March 1987 Vol 111 cc 732–43

18. See appendices 2, 3 and 4.

19. Risk Management Solutions Special Report 2007.

20. The electricity industry calculated a total of 2.3 million 'power disconnection days', a measure that takes the number of disconnected properties and combines it with the length of the disruption. (Report by Professor J. H. Gittus 2004)

21. RMS Special Report 2007.

22. Ghillean Tolmie Prance, director of the Royal Botanic Gardens, Kew 1988–99, knighted in 1995; fellow of the Linnean Society since 1961; fellow of the Royal Society since 1993; awarded the Victoria Medal of Honour in 1999, and the Patron's Gold Medal of the Royal Geographical Society in 1994.

23. *Create Your Own Stage Sets* by Terry Thomas, published by Prentice Hall in 1985.

24. The Garden Festival of Wales was a 1980s initiative by the Conservative government led by Michael Heseltine that sought to inject new life into areas hit by the decline of heavy industry: the reclamation of wasteland for holding festivals, installing playgrounds and other attractions.

25. Designed by the renowned architect Decimus Burton, the grade-I listed Palm House was built between 1844 and 1848 as a home for Kew's tropical plants. It has been restored several times, first in the 1950s, then again in 1985, two years before the storm, when almost the entire building was dismantled: new panes of glass were fitted, its arches strengthened and its ten miles of glazing bars replaced with stainless steel. The Palm House was reopened in 1990.

26. The Countryside Commission ceased to exist in 1999 when it merged with the Rural Development Commission to form the Countryside Agency, which in turn became Natural England in 2006.

27. Dr D. Cutler, Dr P. E. Gasson and Dr M. C. Farmer.

28. There were two questionnaires: Form A for individual trees and Form B for groups of trees of the same species. Dr Farmer and Dr Gasson filled in a high proportion of the A forms, which totalled 886 trees. The B forms, all from correspondents, covered 3,625 trees.

29. *Wilson's China, a Century On* by Mark Flanagan and Tony Kirkham

30. Trees and shrubs found by Wilson in China are catalogued in three volumes: *Plantae Wilsonianae*, published between 1911 and 1917.

31. In his book *When the Wind Blew* (1988), Tony Whitbread, chief executive of the Sussex Wildlife Trust, highlights the post-storm overabundance of the invasive rhododendron: an evergreen shrub from the Himalayas, which thrives on acidic soil, is aggressive, tolerates shade, produces a lot of seed, casts dense shade and supports little wildlife. Sycamore, too – shade tolerant and a prolific producer of seed – has proved invasive. Whitbread notes that woods comprised of ash, oak, beech, wych elm, hazel and maple before the storm have now become sycamore and birch dominant.

32. The Millennium Seed Bank at Wakehurst was opened in 2000. This, the 'greatest concentration of living seed-plant biodiversity on earth', is a 'global resource for conservation and sustainable use of plants'.

33. The Plants and People exhibition opened in the Museum at Kew on 26 May 1998 and was dismantled in May 2016, when the 500 specimens on display returned to the purpose-built storage facilities of the Economic Botany Collection. The EBC was founded by Sir William Hooker, the first director of the Gardens, in April 1841 to illustrate how plant products are used by humans around the world. It has more than a hundred thousand specimens and artefacts, and continues to add at least a thousand items each year. It has been and is a key resource for historians of medicine, science, exploration and empire in the last 175 years.

34. For the seventy years between 1645 and 1715, it was as if a dark curtain had been drawn across the sun over parts of Europe and

North America, as prolonged and bitter winters brought heavy snow-falls that stayed on the ground for months. This Arctic period came in the middle of the Little Ice Age, which lasted in the northern hemisphere from about 1500 to 1850, during which pack ice in the North Atlantic began to march south and glaciers expanded world-wide. There were snowstorms in Lisbon; farmers in the Swiss Alps watched their mountain meadows turn to ice fields; from London to Amsterdam, rivers and canals froze, people learned to skate, knitted themselves extra layers and held winter festivals and frost fairs on the floe. Springs and summers brought fierce storms and severe floods and large tracts of the low-lying Danish, German and Dutch coasts were lost forever.

35. The cellist Jacqueline du Pré shot to worldwide fame in the late sixties with her uninhibited, virtuosic performances on the Davidov Stradivarius, made by Stradivari in 1712. In 1970, however, she rejected the Davidov in favour of a more modern cello, saying that the instrument, given to her by her godmother, was 'unpredictable'. When she was only twenty-eight years old, du Pré was diagnosed with multiple sclerosis and forced to stop playing. She died fourteen years later, paralysed, mute and blind.

The priceless Davidov, now owned by the Vuitton Foundation, is currently on loan to the cellist Yo-Yo Ma who, when asked for his thoughts on why du Pré may have found it unsuitable, said, 'Jackie's unbridled dark qualities went against the Davidov. You have to coax the instrument. The more you attack it, the less it returns.'

Du Pré died on 19 October 1987, but in the controversial film about her life, *Hilary and Jackie*, directed by Anand Tucker, her death was brought forward by three days for dramatic effect to coincide with the night of the Great Storm.
http://stringsmagazine.com/how-jacqueline-du-pre-sparked-a-cello-explosion/
http://www.newsday.co.tt/sport/0,60124.html

36. *A Sand County Almanac and Sketches Here and There* by Aldo Leopold (p. 68 Oxford University Press, 1949)

37. In 2016, the Forestry Commission confirmed that 13 per cent of the total land area in the UK was covered by woodland, compared

to Europe's 37 per cent: one of the aims of a report commissioned by the Independent Panel on Forestry in 2012 was to increase that UK figure to 15 per cent by 2060, taking England back to a level of woodland last recorded in the Domesday Book in 1086. With the nation's renewed interest in trees and in the spirit of recovery in the first few years after the storm, there was a boom in tree planting, and although the rate has slowed in the past few years, the woodland area in the country has risen, with both new trees and restocking, by around two hundred and forty thousand hectares since 1998.

38. A series of photographic books such as *In the Wake of the Hurricane*, compiled by the newspaper editor Bob Ogley, who hired a light aircraft and flew over storm-damaged Britain in the days after.

39. About a seventh of the total number of trees in Britain.

40. The Dartford warbler was given its distinctly Kentish name after a mating pair were discovered dead in Bexleyheath in 1773.

41. *The London Bird Report* 1987.

42. An ornithological 'wreck' is when large numbers of seabirds are driven inland due to adverse weather.

43. Forestry Commission top tree diseases: https://www.forestry.gov.uk

44. The Ashmead's Kernel was described on Radio 4 in 1944 by the wine and food writer Morton Shand, thus: 'What an apple, what suavity of aroma. Its initial Madeira-like mellowness of flavour overlies a deeper honeyed nuttiness, crisply sweet not sugar sweet, but the succulence of a well devilled marrow bone. Surely no apple of greater distinction or more perfect balance can ever have been raised anywhere on earth.'

45. In 2005, the People's Trust for Endangered Species launched a campaign to save the aristocratically named noble chafer, a reclusive beetle with an iridescent green shell, whose larvae like to gorge on the decaying heartwood of mature fruit trees, before emerging to live their short but sparkling life in the scented canopy. The noble chafer once lived in old trees all over the fruit-growing counties of

Gloucestershire, Herefordshire and Worcestershire and though still rare, happily, with the awareness raised by the campaign, a population of noble chafers has been found in Kent, where they had not been reported for over sixty years.

46. Formed in 1983 by Sue Clifford, Angela King and the writer Roger Deakin, Common Ground finds ways to engage people with their local communities and environment through creative and social projects.

47. A fairlead is a ring, hook or structure mounted on a boat to guide the towrope and to stop it rubbing against another surface.

48. Emergency tows are strapped to the sides of the ship under tow, and attached to a rope on a buoy that trails fifty yards behind, facilitating the recapture of the ship after the main tow has parted.

49. The Loran C was another hyberbolic navigation system that determines sea or air position based on the difference in timing between the reception of two signals.

50. A sextant is a navigation instrument that measures the angle between the horizon and a celestial body or astronomical object.

51. 'The Listeners', a poem by Walter de la Mare (1873–1956).

52. The Cornish pilot gig, a six-oared rowing boat built of Cornish narrow leaf elm, was once a working vessel that ferried pilots offshore to collect incoming Atlantic vessels. In the late seventeenth century gigs were also used as lifeboats, but they are now mainly used for racing.

53. Sydney Harbour is the deepest natural harbour in the world, the Port of Mahon in Menorca the second deepest and Falmouth the third.

54. Gladys was descended from the legendary fishwife Mary Kelynack who, in 1851 at the age of eighty-four, walked three hundred miles from Newlyn to London to see the Great Exhibition. At the end of her remarkably well-publicised five-week journey Mary was introduced to Queen Victoria and Prince Albert, had tea with the Mayor and had her portrait carved by the renowned Cornish sculptor,

Neville Northey Burnard, at which point, apparently, she had burst into tears and asked for a lift home. Mary was the subject of a Radio 4 *Ramblings* programme in 2012.

55. Terry played in the back row of the scrum for Falmouth Rugby Club and, when the County Championship was second only to playing for England, he played for his county, Cornwall, twenty-five times.

56. Dennis Mills, a member of the Joint Services School for Linguists 1951–60, described my father as 'a rare bird': one of a very small number of Royal Navy intercept operators trained before the main Cold War effort in 1950 (most were from the RAF) who served in the Baltic with Commander Harvey Jones (later a prominent businessman) on secret work that involved landing agents as well as interception.

57. *Hurricane Force* by George Hill (Collins)

58. 'Pitmatic', also known as 'pitmatical' or 'yakka', was a dialect developed by miners in the Northumberland and Durham coalfields.

59. Although the official school-leaving age was raised to fourteen in 1921, many children, particularly in industrial areas or mining towns, left early to contribute to a family's household income. The school-leaving age was raised to fifteen in 1947 and to sixteen in 1973.

60. Hundreds of Shetland ponies, specially bred for the job on the Isle of Bressay, were shipped to Seaham by boat, many of them spending their entire lives in underground stables, hauling props and tubs of coal from the deepest seams. Horses were employed from the earliest days of mining, sometimes travelling up to twenty-five miles a day underground for sixty hours a week. They were used on a large scale after the gap in manpower left by the Mines Act 1842, the change in the law that abolished the employment of children under ten and women.

61. The romantic poet Lord Byron married Annabella, the only daughter of Sir Ralph Milbanke, lord of the manor, and lived at Seaham Hall between 1815 and 1816.

62. A coble is a flat-bottomed, high-bowed traditional fishing boat, developed in the north-east, which allows for launching and landing from shallow sandy beaches.

63. 'Asylum by Ordeal' by David Burgess, *New Law Journal* (1991), vol 131, issue 8487.